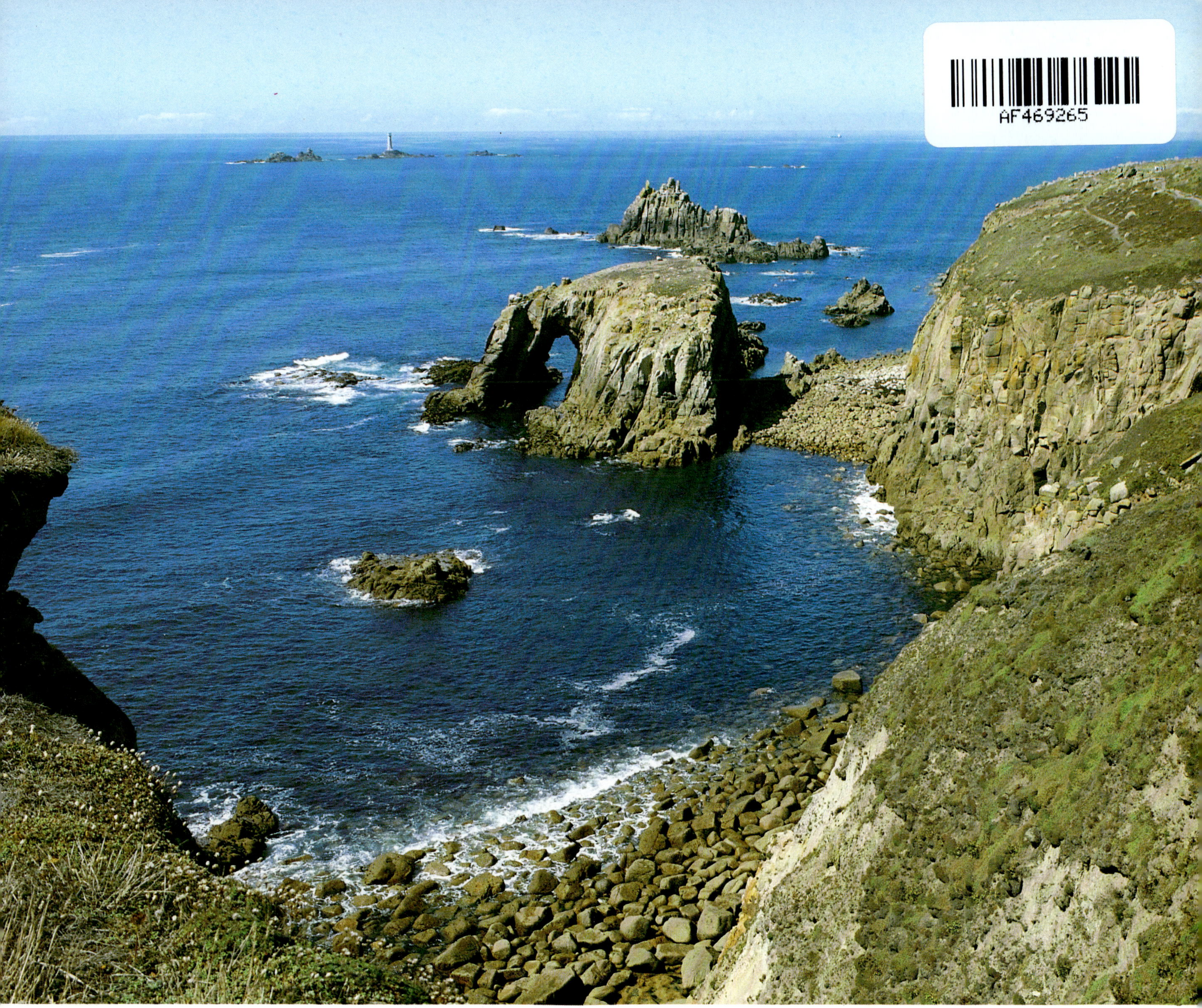

Land's End. Battered by waves and Atlantic gales the spectacular granite cliffs of Land's End, steeped in ancient lore and legend, form England's most westerly point. Among the bizarre rock forms which can be seen offshore are the Armed Knight and Enys Dodman while the Longships Lighthouse stands more than a mile away warning of the wild and forbidding cliffs.

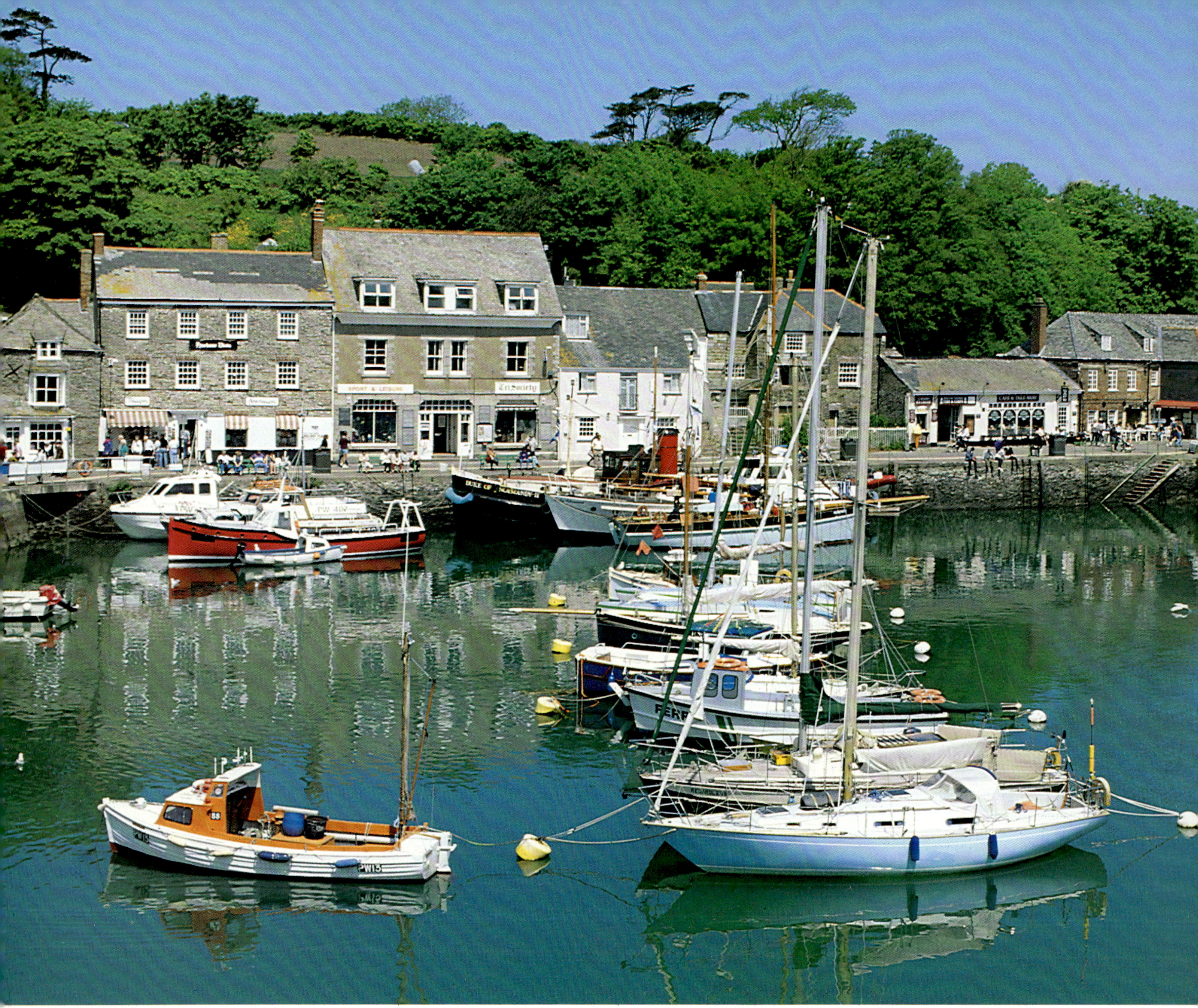

Padstow Quay. With its picturesque harbour and bustling quayside, Padstow stands on the western side of the River Camel estuary. This ancient little fishing port, which can trace its origins back to the 6th century, is the gateway to some of Cornwall's loveliest bays and the harbour was once one of the busiest on the North Cornwall coast handling cargoes as diverse as fish, wine, slate and ore.

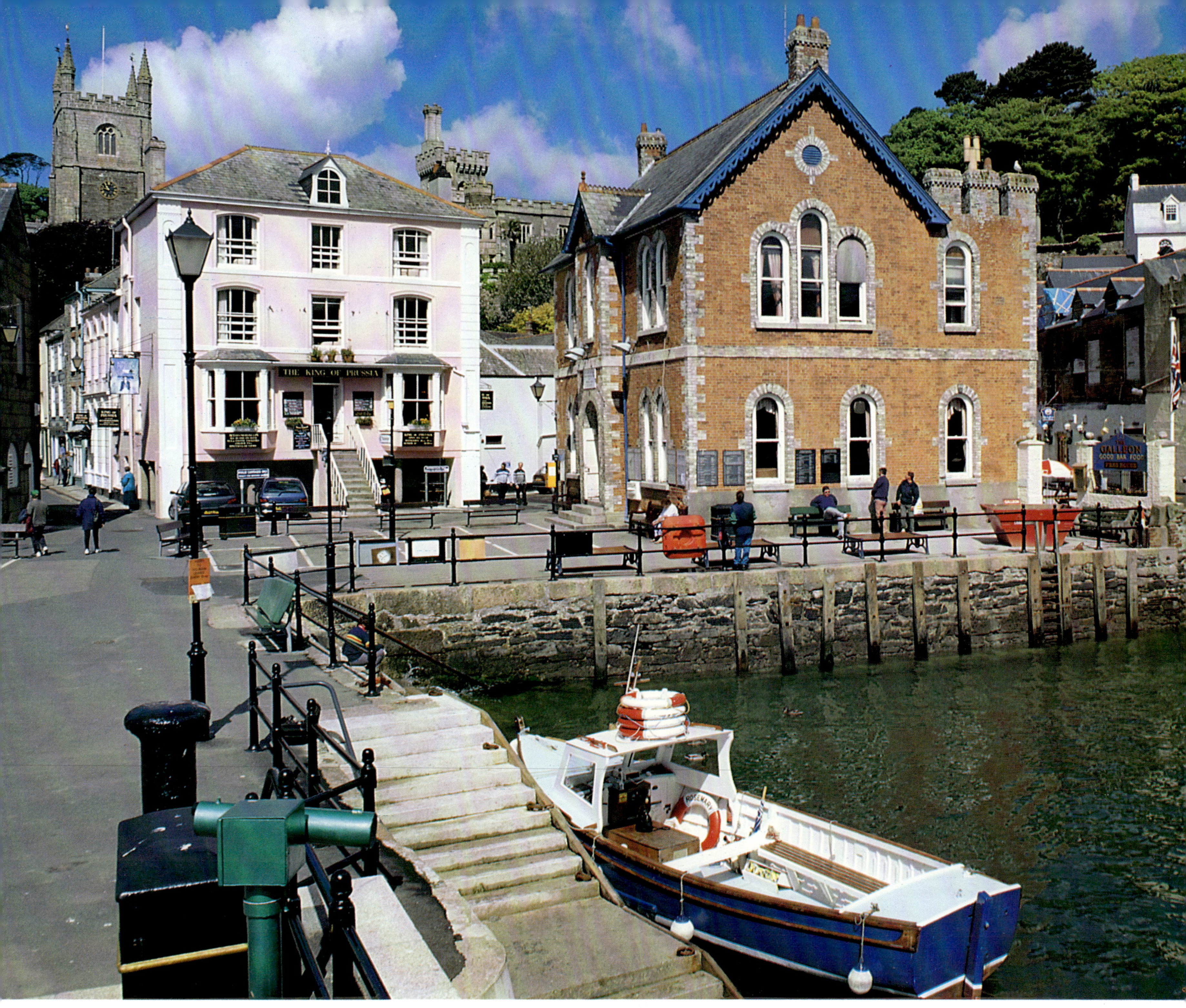

Town Quay, Fowey. The sheltered waters of Fowey's fine natural harbour have made it a busy port since the Middle Ages. An inlet sandwiched between imposing wooded headlands, it provides safe anchorage for hundreds of yachts in the summer months and Town Quay is always a busy and colourful scene of activity with all manner of craft visiting the town for both business and pleasure.

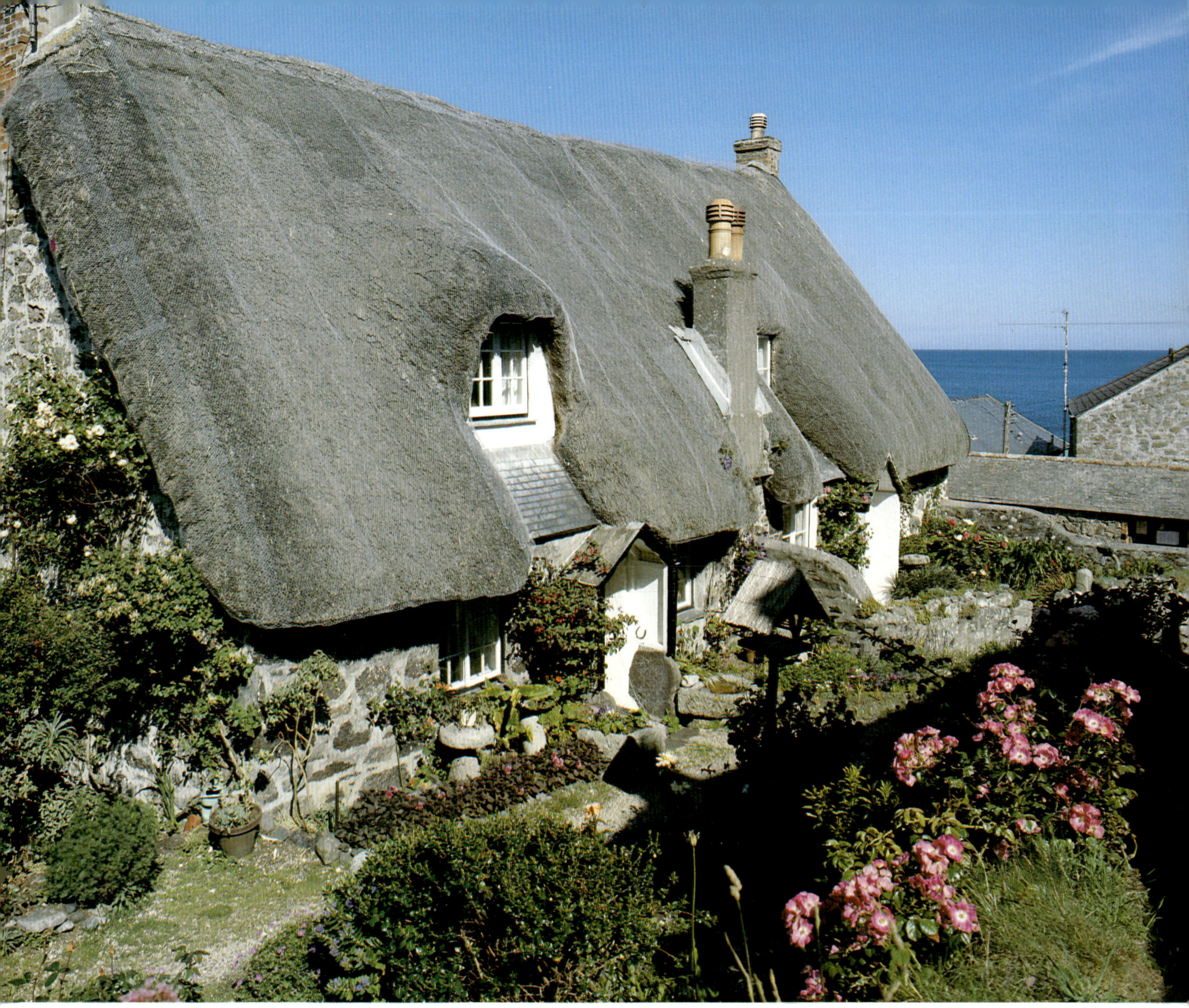

Cadgwith. Known for its rocky coastline and delightful sandy coves, the Lizard Peninsula has some of the finest scenery in the country. The area also abounds in sturdy thatched cottages and this attractive example stands in the unspoilt village of Cadgwith which lies at the foot of a steep and heavily wooded valley tucked between rocky headlands on the eastern side of the peninsula.

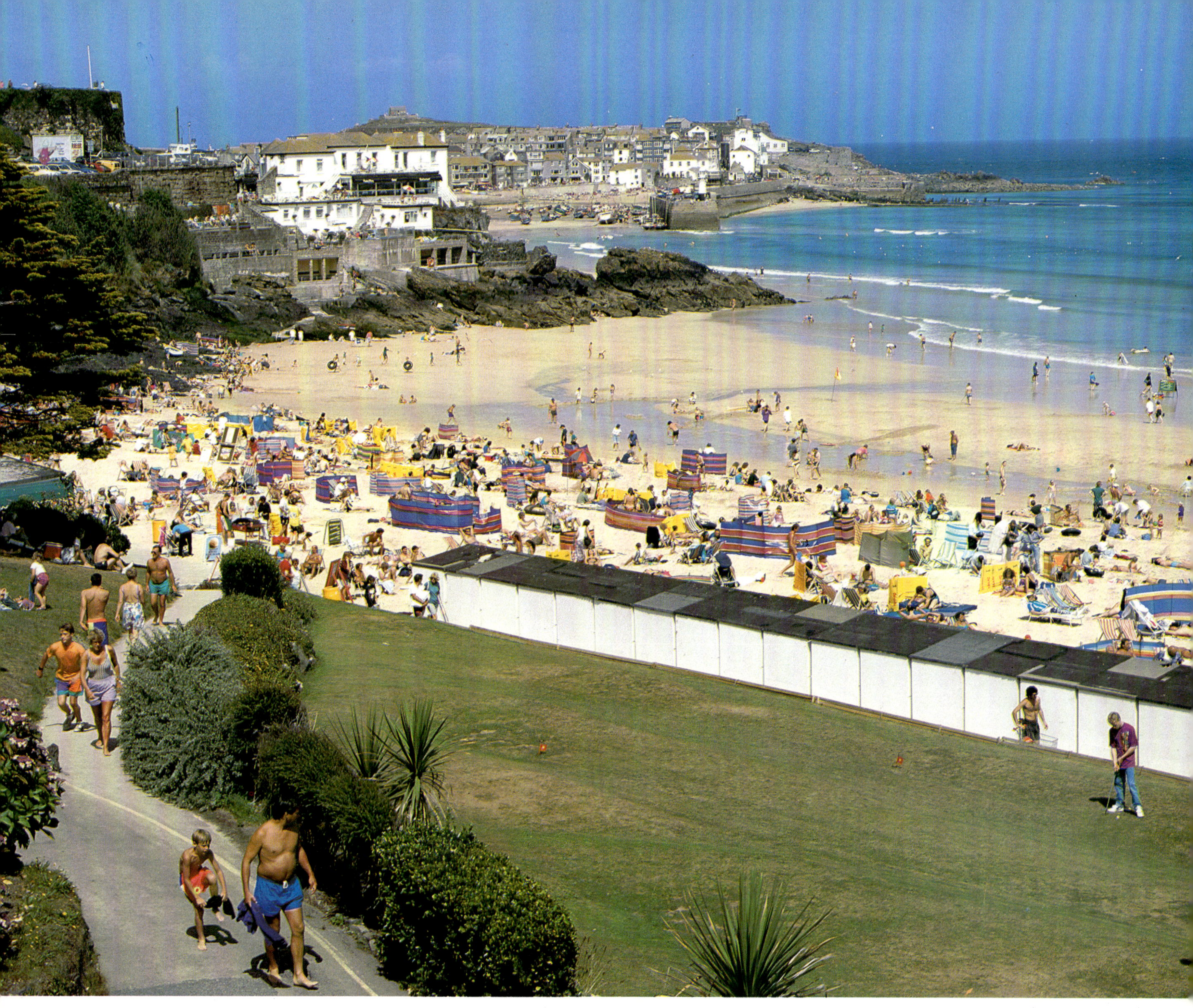

Porthminster Beach, St. Ives. Situated on the north coast of the peninsula, the fine beaches of St. Ives Bay are as popular with summer visitors as are the quaint streets of old St. Ives with artists. Backed by attractive lawns and gardens, the long golden sands of Porthminster Beach provide some of the best bathing in the county sheltered as they are by St. Ives Head.

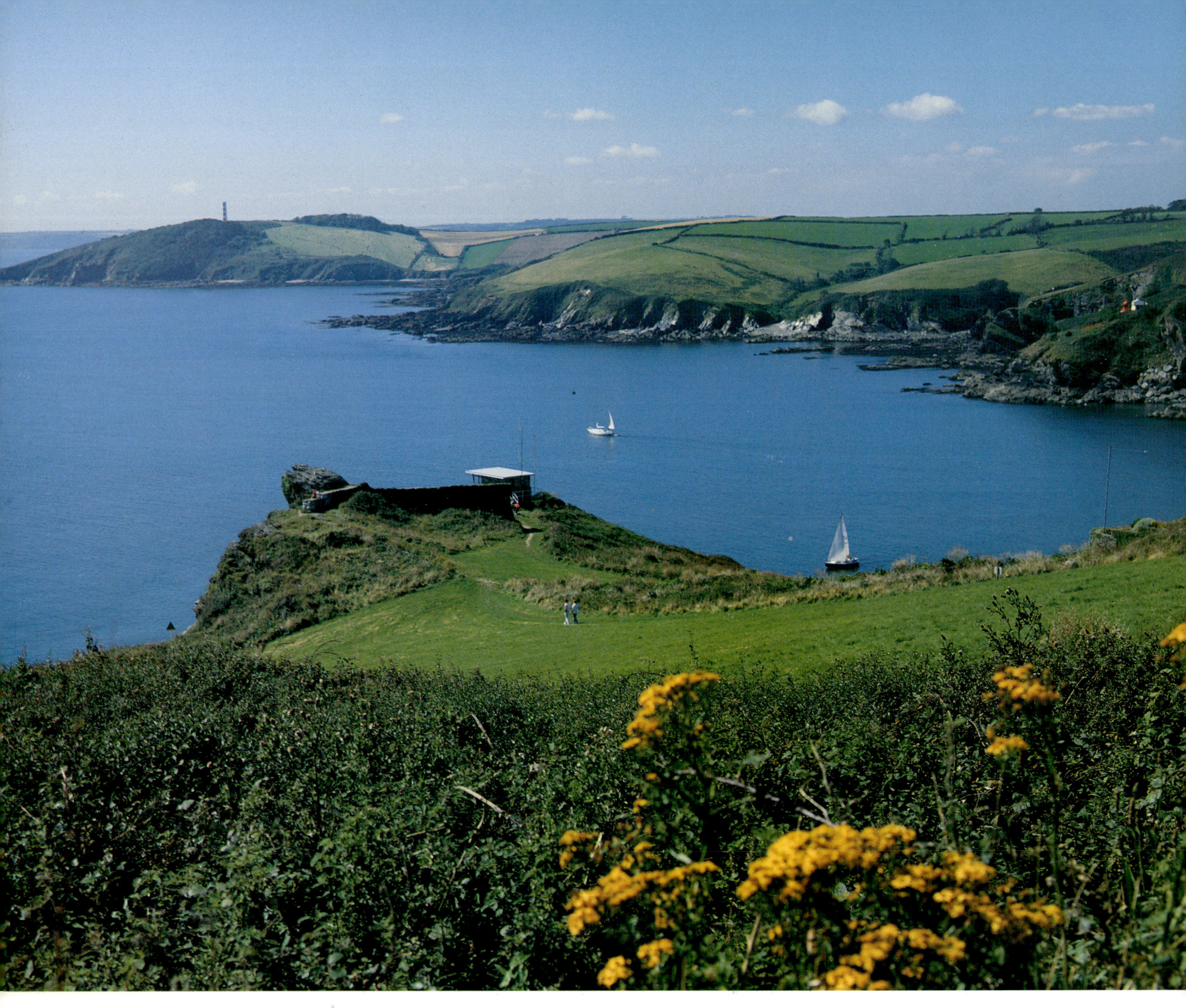

Gribbin Head. Seen here from Polruan, across the estuary of the Fowey River, Gribbin Head juts into the sea at the eastern end of St. Austell Bay. From the summit of this craggy headland, where a beacon 84 feet high was erected in 1832 as an aid to sailors, there are superb views which extend on a clear day from Dodman Point in the west as far as Rame Head to the east.

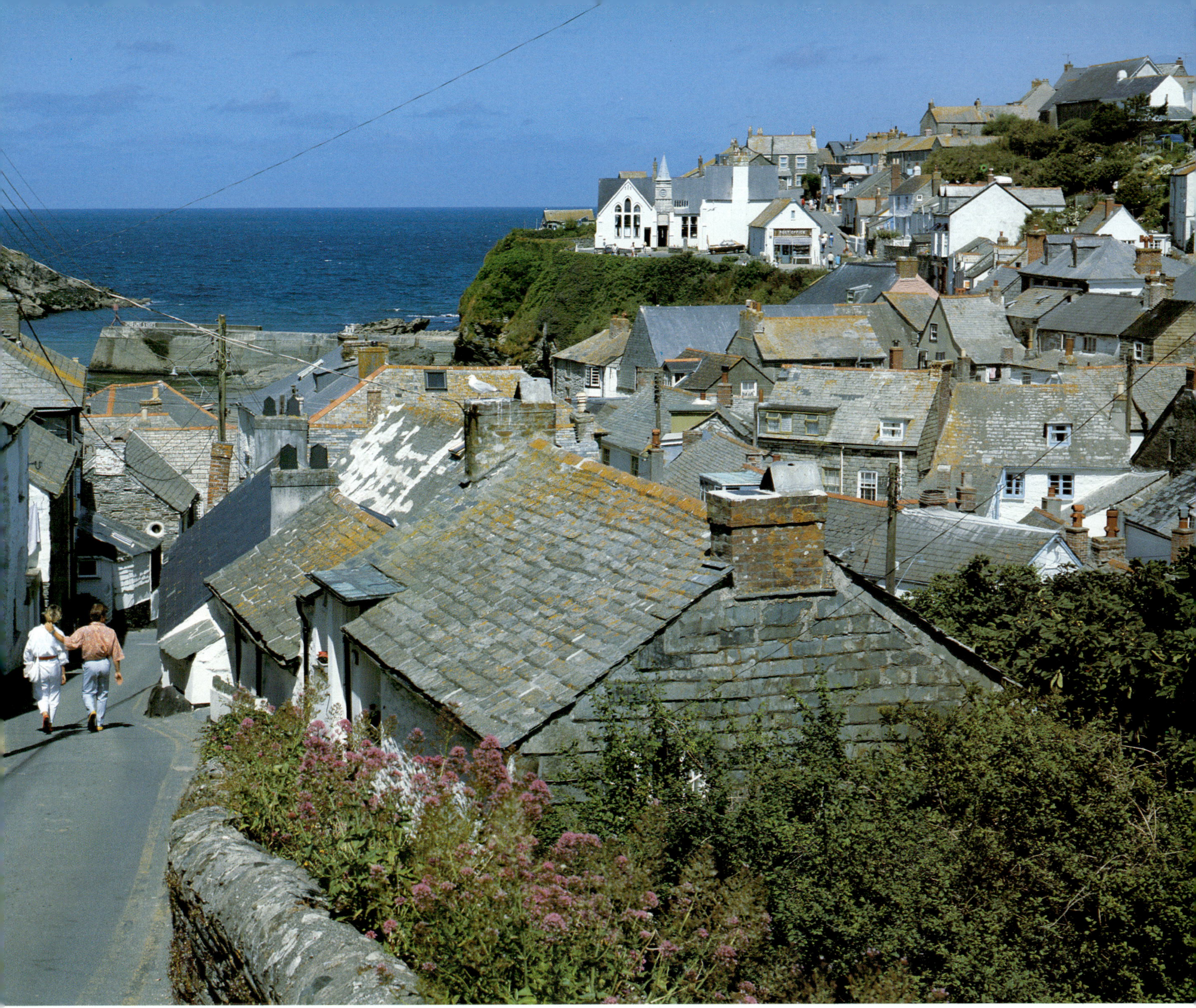

Port Isaac. The tiny haven of Port Isaac, nestling in a break in the rugged coastline between Padstow and Tintagel is one of the most picturesque of Cornwall's many fishing villages. Among the steep streets and narrow passageways lined with slate-hung white-painted cottages is precipitious Church Hill which leads down to the harbour with its boats, nets and lobster pots.

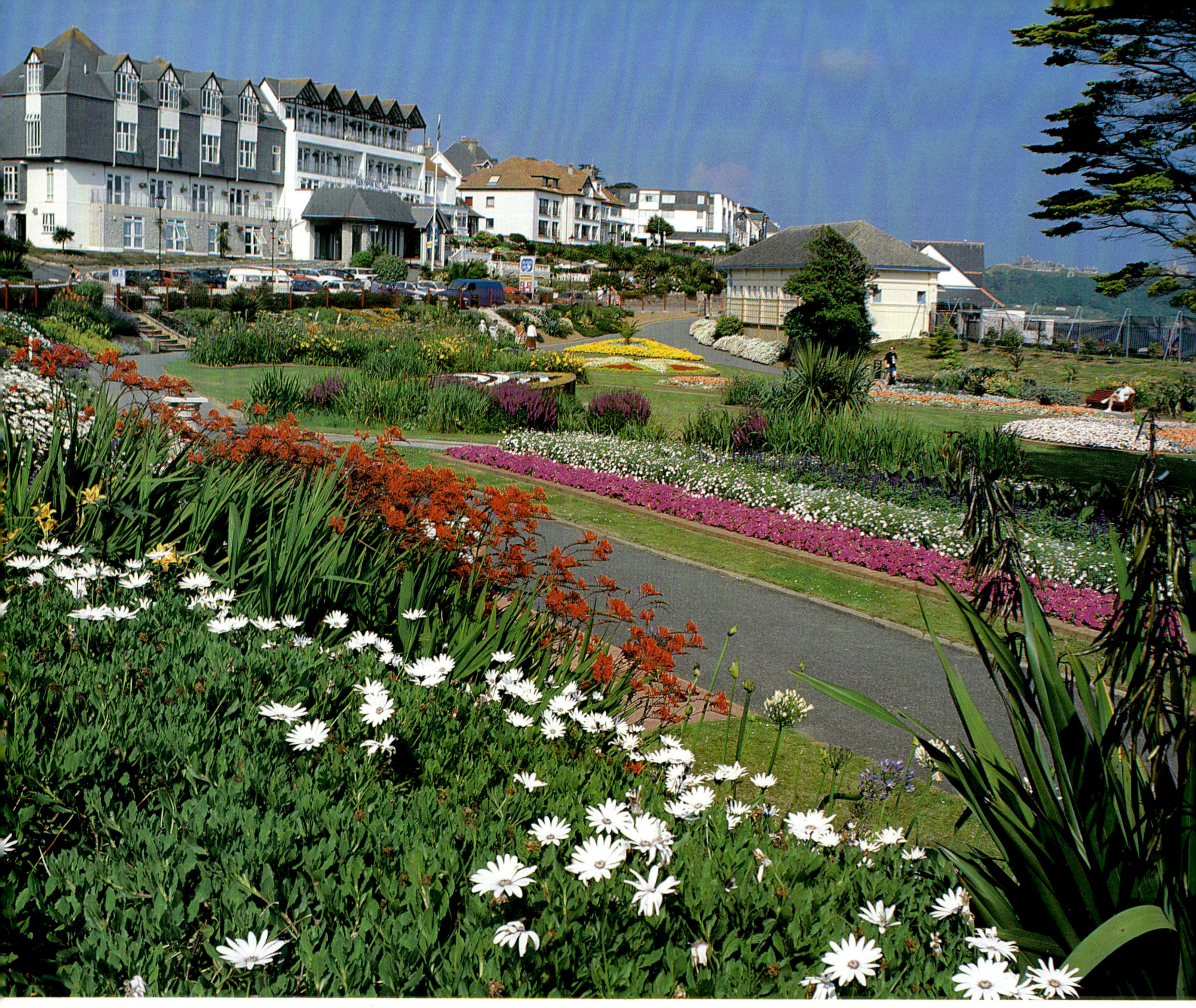

Queen Mary Gardens, Falmouth. A modern resort which combines every sort of scenic beauty, Falmouth stands at the mouth of the lovely River Fal overlooking a bay indented with picturesque inlets. Backed by wooded hills it has a climate so temperate that palm trees line its streets and the attractive Queen Mary Gardens provide a blaze of colour on the promenade.

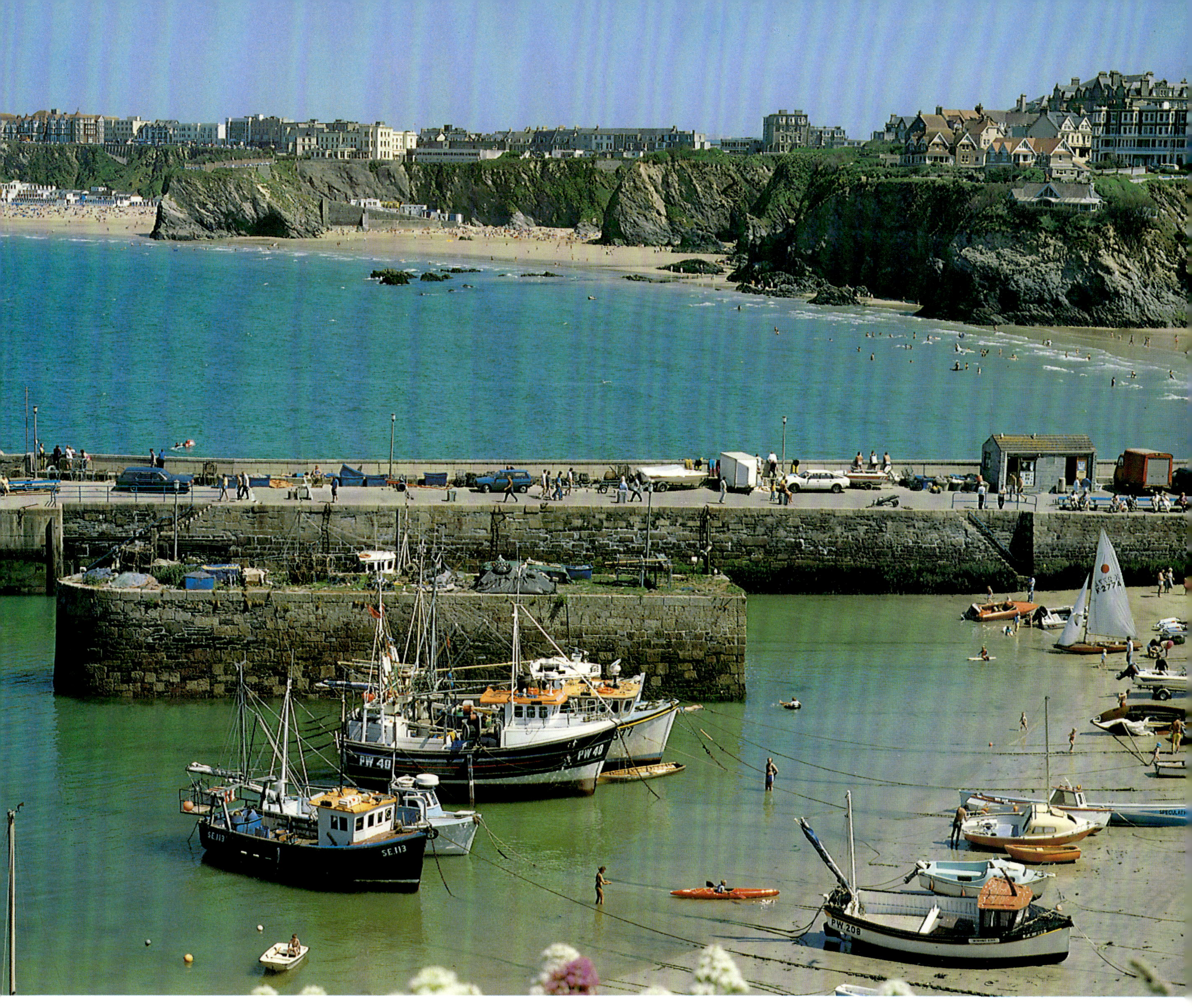

Newquay Harbour. Although it is Cornwall's largest holiday resort and Britain's main surfing centre, Newquay is an ancient town and the "new quay" from which it takes its name probably dates from the 15th century. It retains much of its character as an old fishing and trading port and the harbour, which dries out at low tide to provide another beach, is well used by small boats.

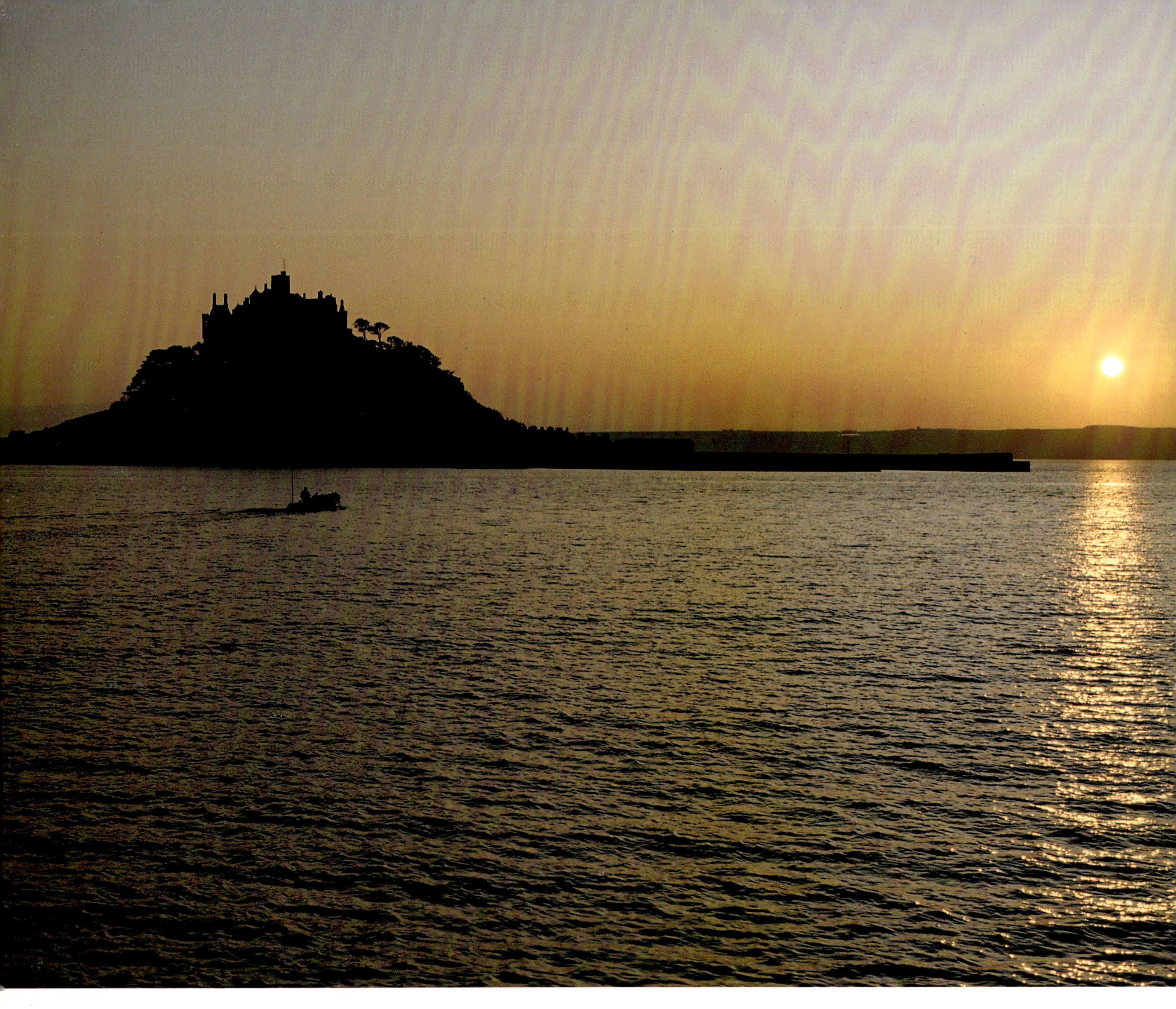

St. Michael's Mount. Connected to the mainland by a stone causeway which is only accessible at low tide, this rocky pyramid rises nearly 300 feet from the waters of Mount's Bay opposite the ancient town of Marazion. It was originally the site of a Benedictine priory established by Edward the Confessor but is now topped by a spectacular 14th century castle.

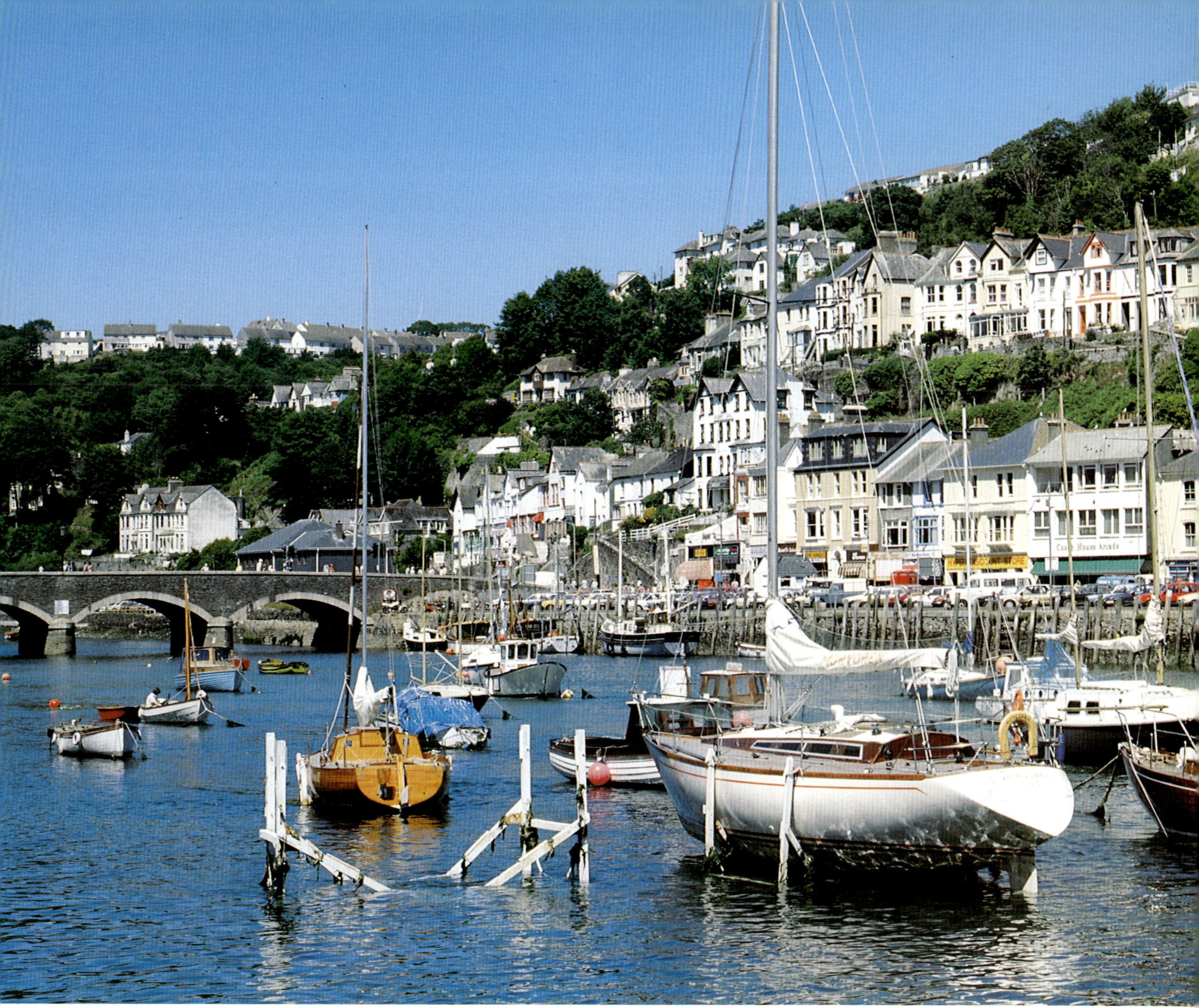

Looe. The ancient towns of East and West Looe are built on either side of the deep valley of the Looe River, sandwiched between precipitious hills and linked by a handsome many-arched bridge. The harbour is popular with both fishermen and holiday-makers and the busy river, which divides into two streams as it wanders inland, is always thronged with small craft.

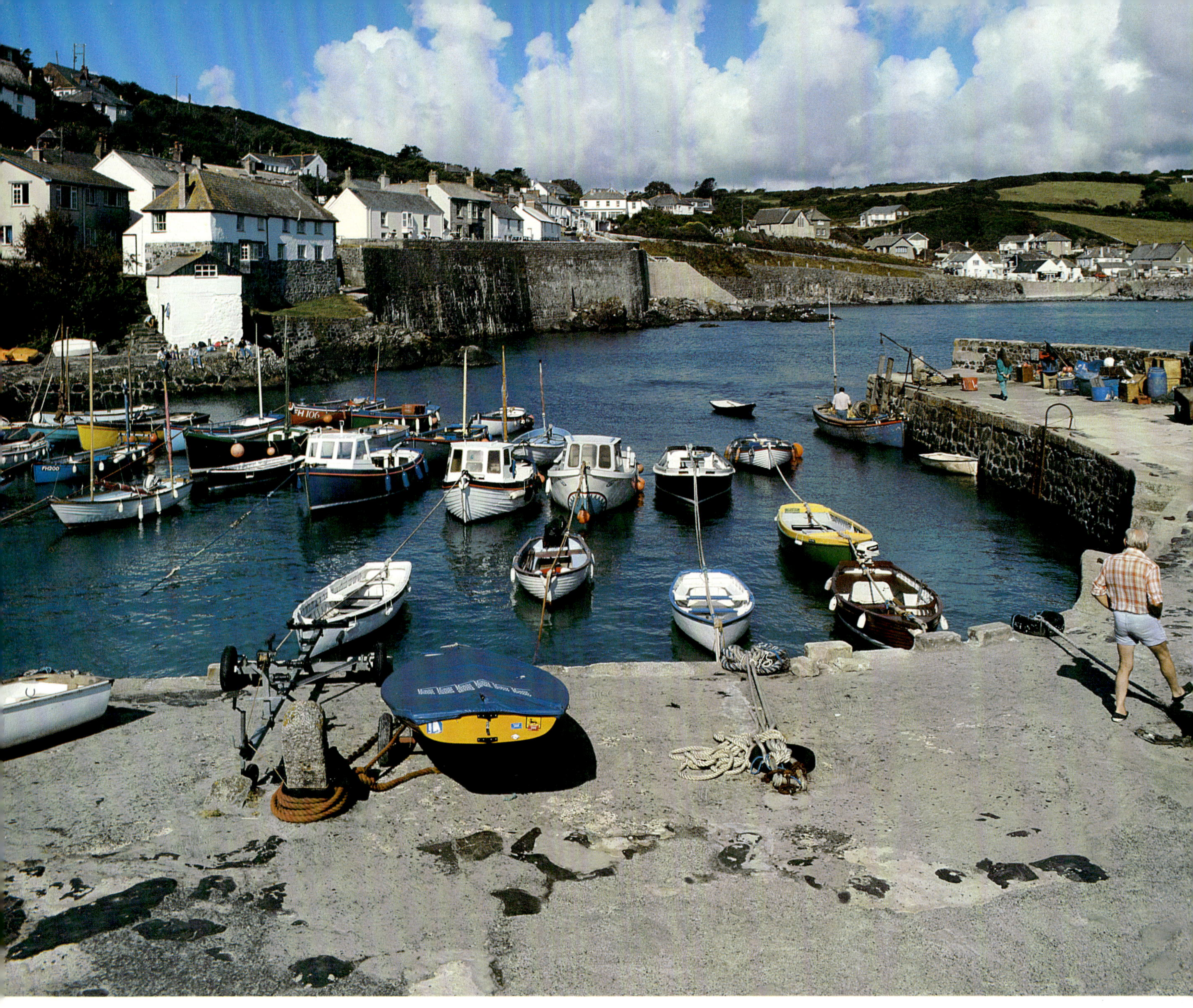

Coverack Harbour. The picturesque fishing village of Coverack lies under the shelter of Black Head on the eastern side of the Lizard peninsula. Now popular with summer visitors it was once well known for its smuggling activities and the small harbour has for centuries provided a refuge for fishermen on this exposed stretch of coast with its dangerous offshore rocks

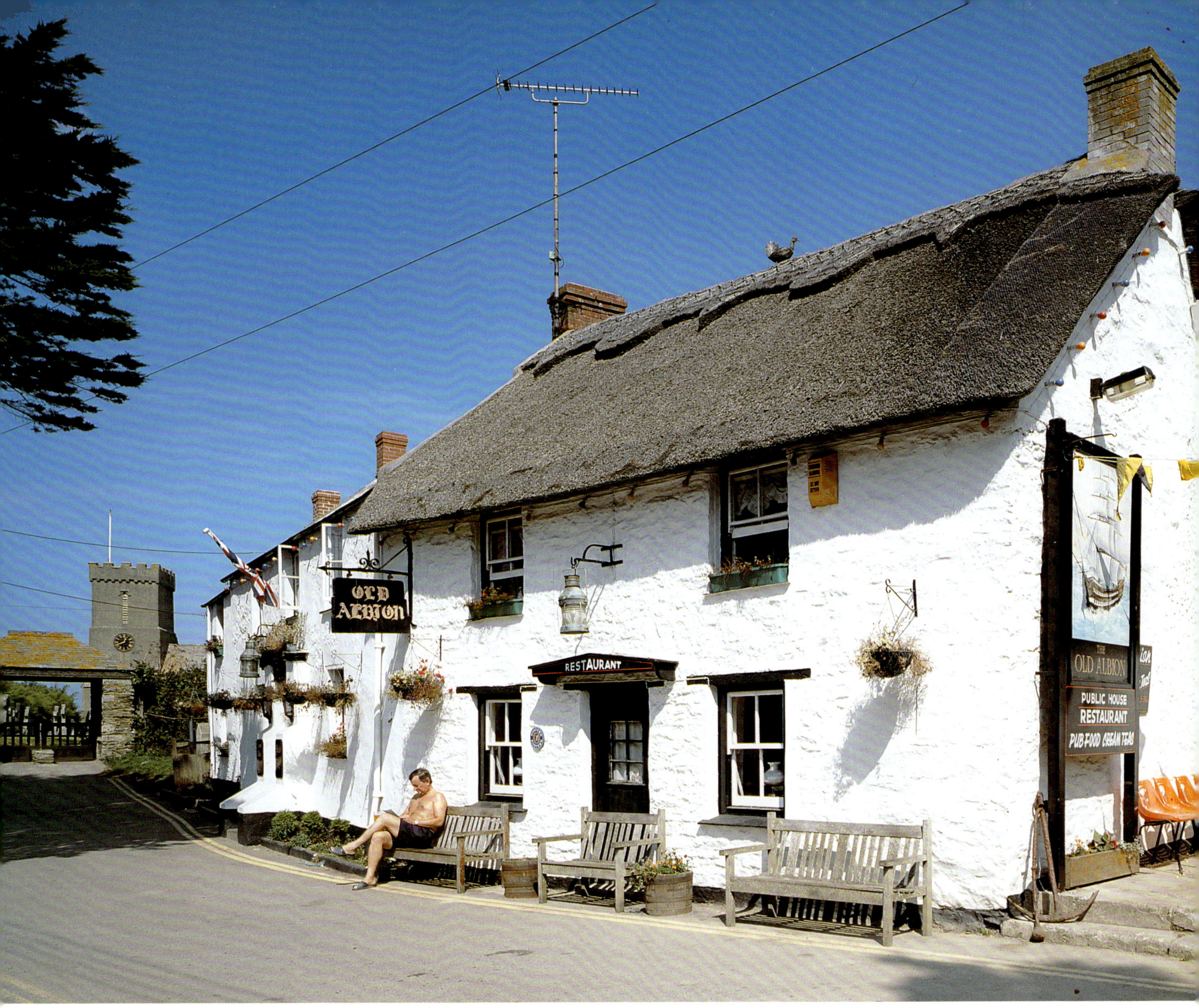

Old Albion Inn, Crantock. Set amongst beautiful surroundings on the southern side of the sandy Gannel estuary is the pretty village of Crantock, its colour-washed cottages clustered around a tiny square. At one time it boasted three inns, but they were closed in Victorian times owing to the influence of the Temperance movement and only the charming, thatched Old Albion Inn has re-opened.

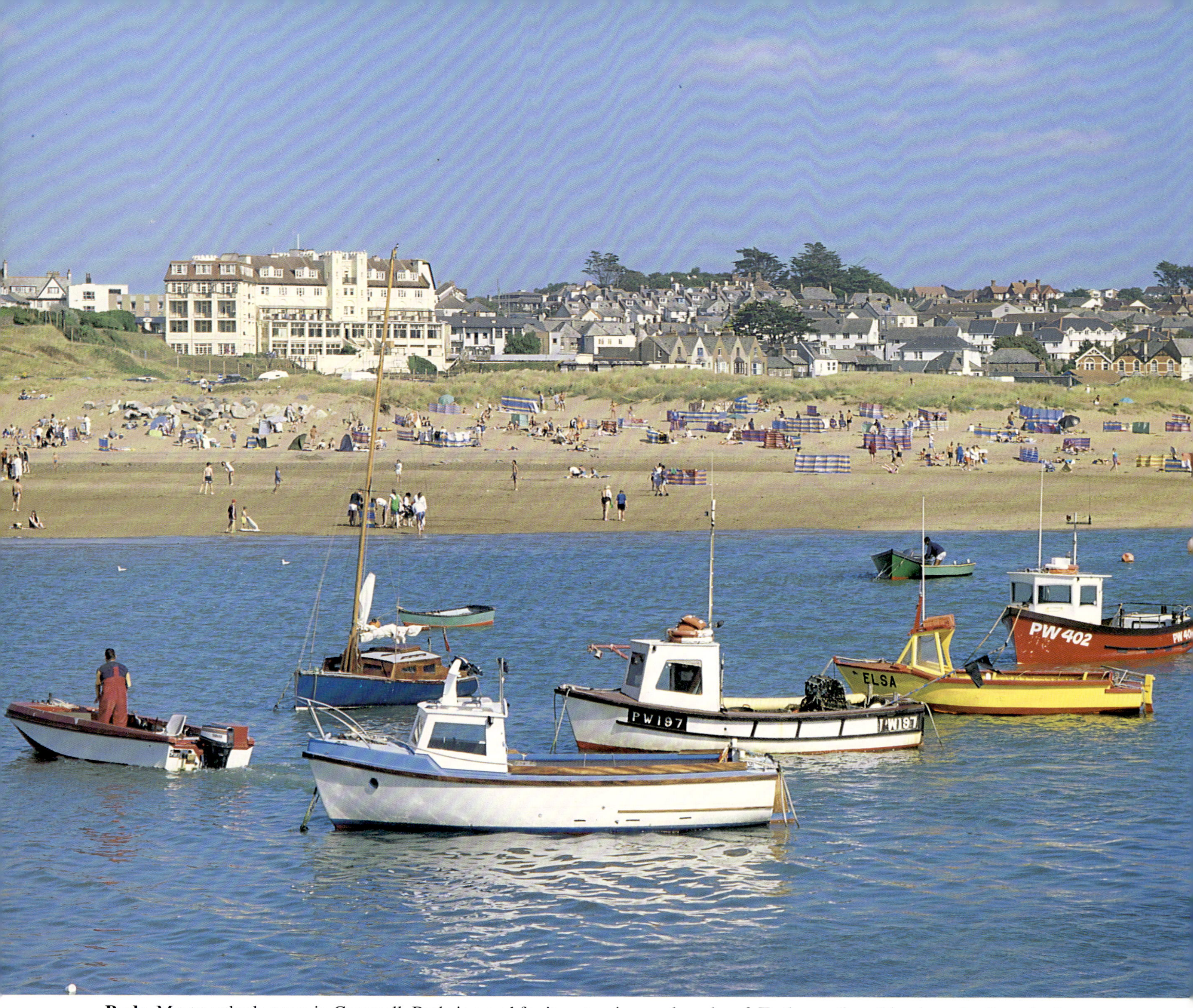

Bude. Most northerly town in Cornwall, Bude is noted for its extensive sands and surf. To the south nothing impedes the relentless surge of the Atlantic rollers onto the beaches which have become popular with surfers from all over the world. Surrounded by magnificent cliff scenery, the modern holiday town of Bude makes an excellent centre for exploring the local countryside.

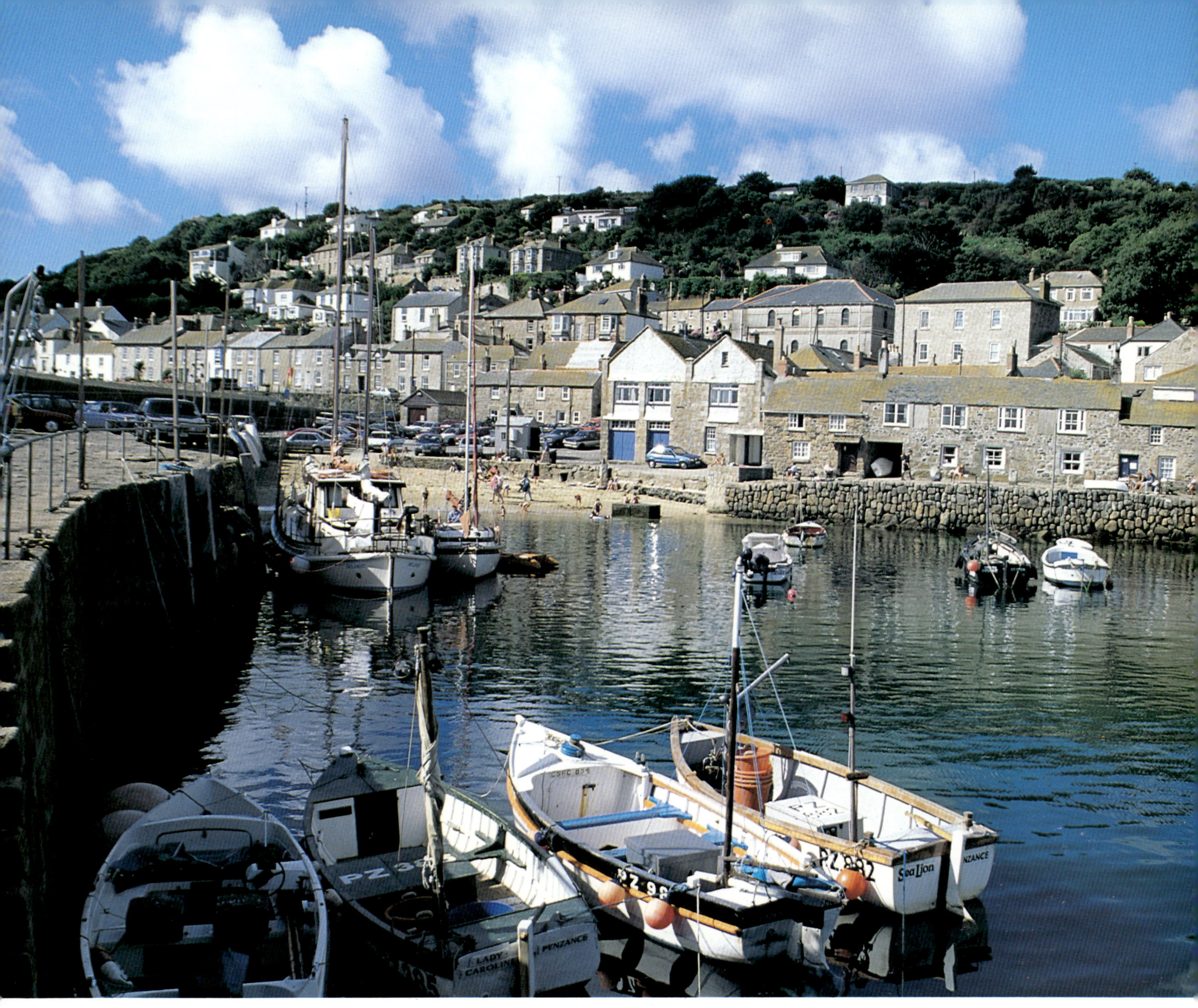

Mousehole. The fishing village of Mousehole lies in a valley two miles south of Newlyn. Visited by Phoenician tin merchants more than 2500 years ago, the village has a long history and many quaint old cottages are crowded into the narrow streets around the harbour. It was here that Dolly Pentreath died in 1777, the last person known to use the Cornish language as her native tongue.

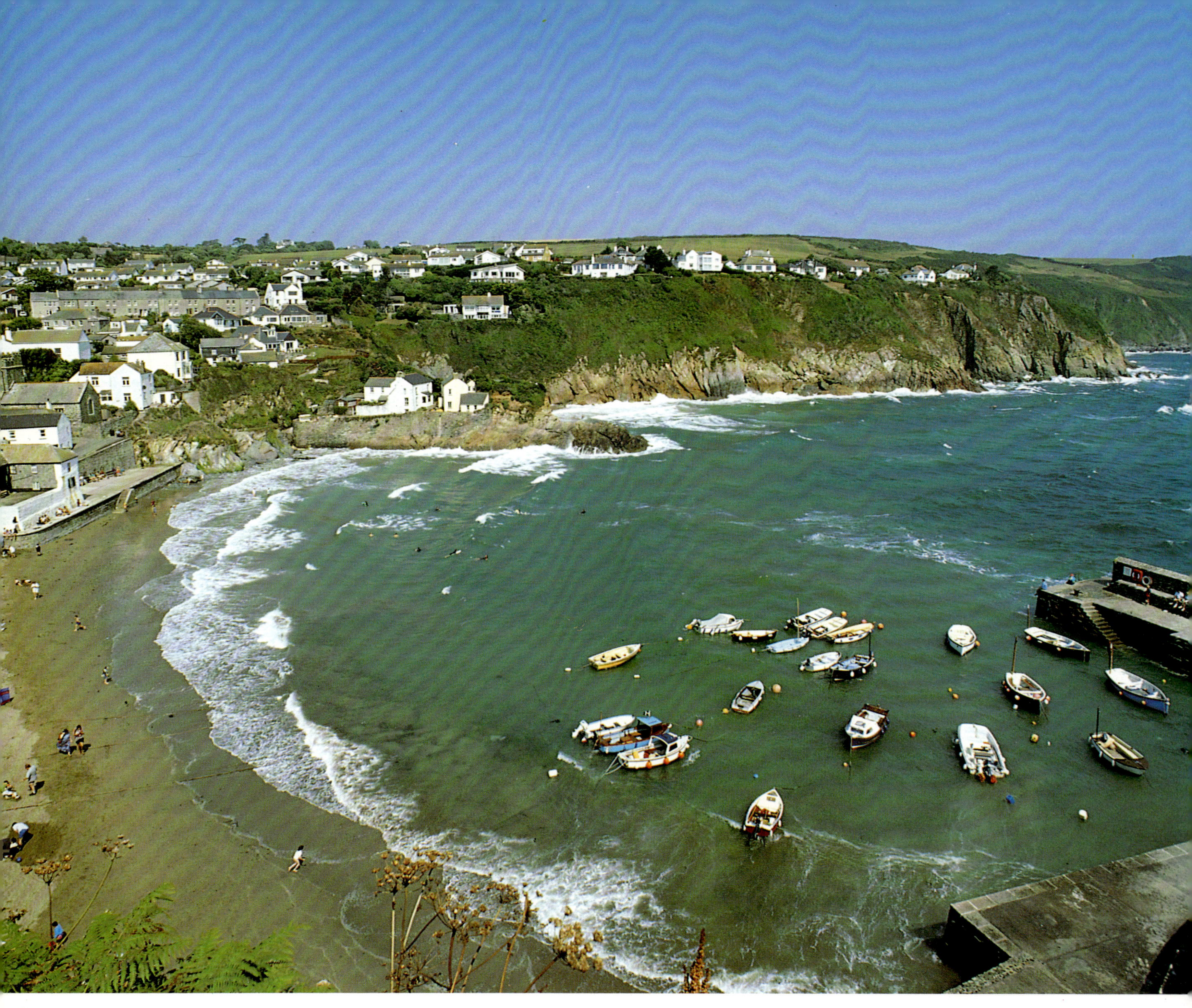

Gorran Haven. Due north of Dodman Point, a major landmark on Cornwall's southern coast and the cause of many ship-wrecks, is the former fishing hamlet of Gorran Haven. Now a popular resort it has a small sandy beach sheltered at one end by an arm of the cliff. The little stone quay is used by fishermen and from the village there is a fine coastal path around the bay.

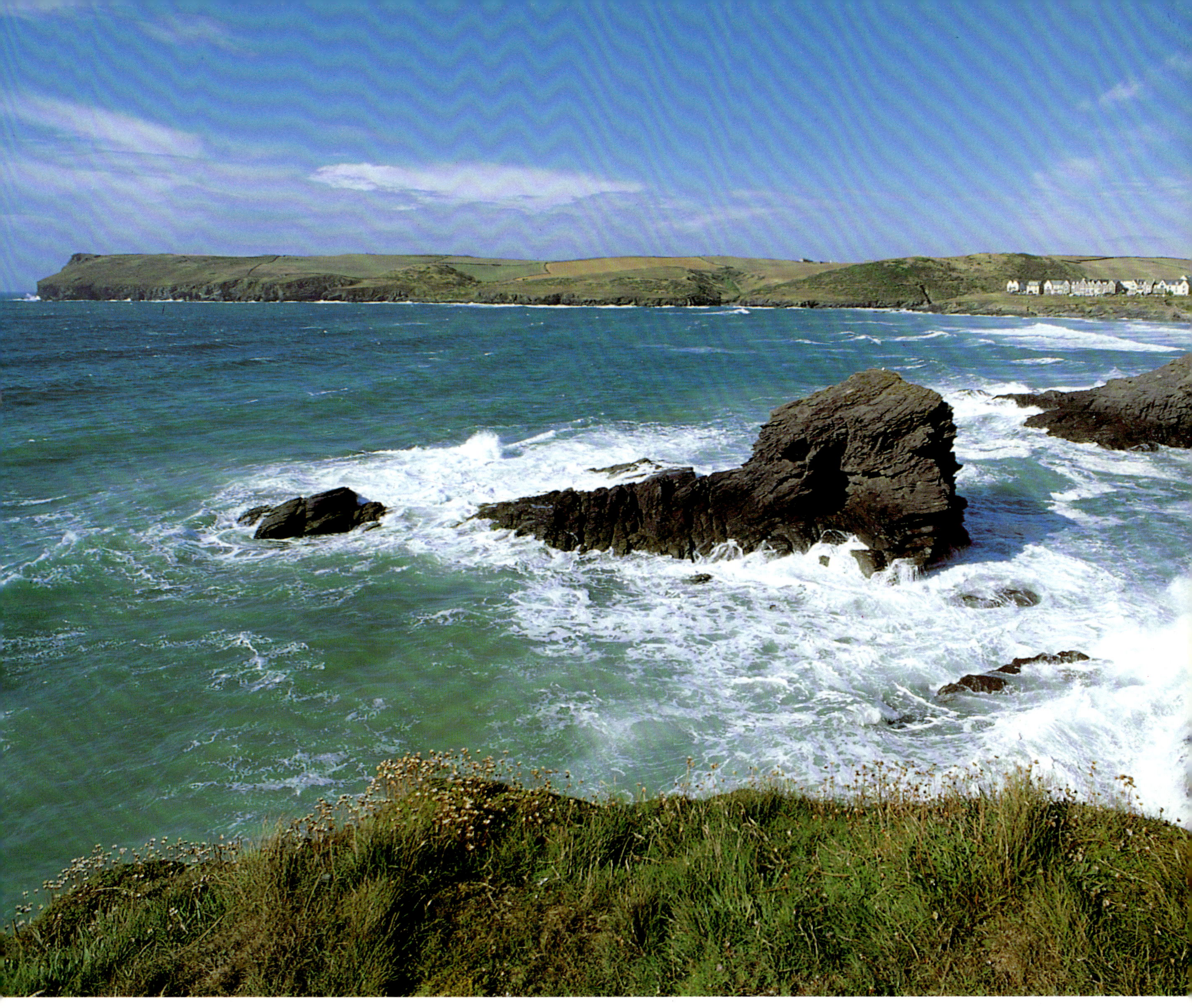

Polzeath. The resort of Polzeath, a village at the head of Hayle Bay in the Camel estuary to the north of Padstow, is growing in popularity. It has a fine expanse of sand with rocks and is sheltered by nearby Pentire Point. About a mile to the south is the ancient Church of St. Enodoc which at one time was almost entirely engulfed by sand but later reclaimed and restored.

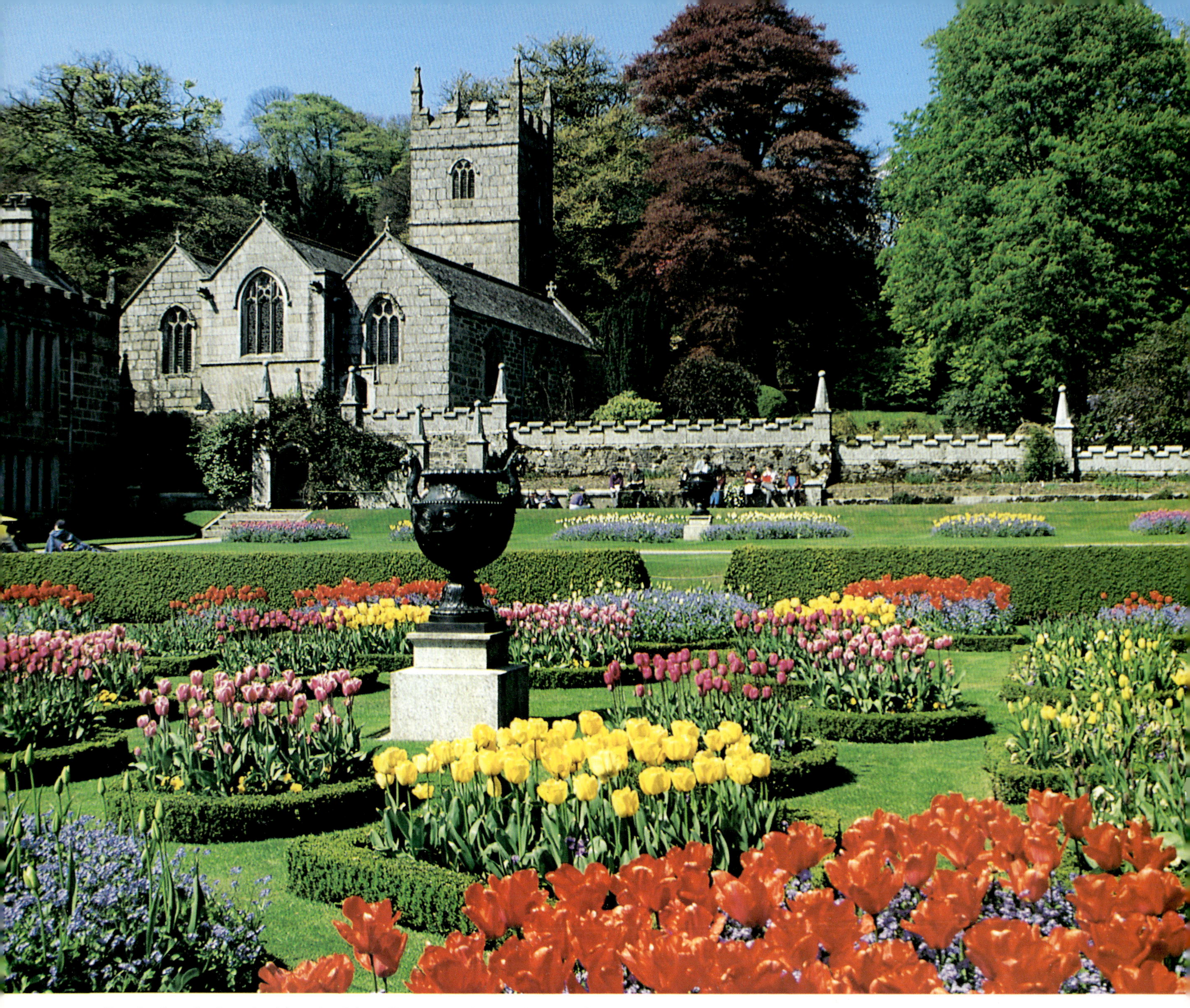

Lanhydrock. Overlooking the River Fowey to the south east of Bodmin, the little Church of St. Hydrock stands in the beautiful wooded parkland which is attached to Lanhydrock House. Mature trees and rare shrubs, flourishing in the mild climate, surround this splendid Jacobean mansion and there is also a fine formal garden which consists of lawns, rosebeds and clipped yews.

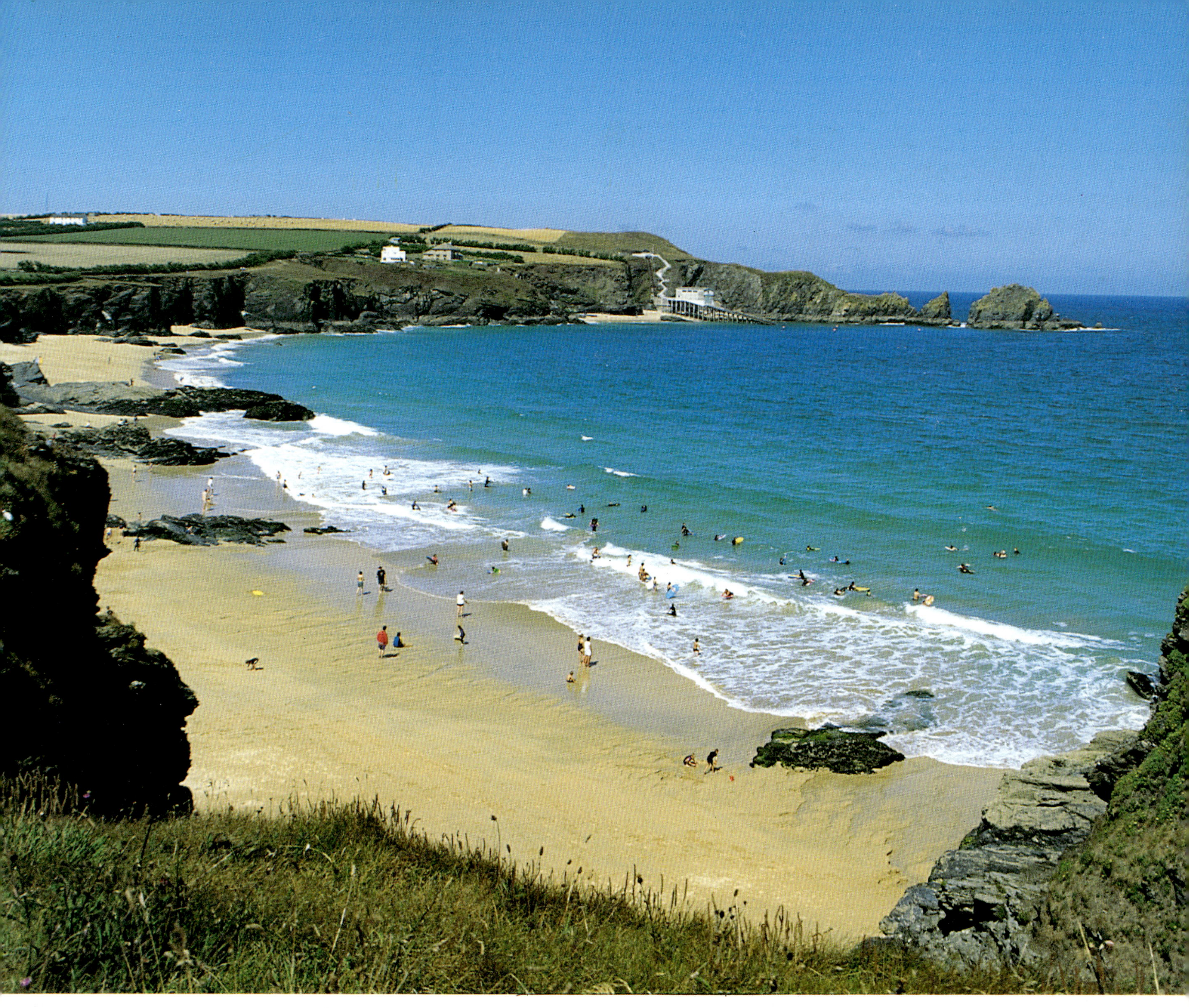

Mother Ivey's Bay. Said to take its name from a local woman who claimed any wreckage found on the shore, this sandy little cove lies on the sheltered eastern side of Trevose Head. The grassy summit of the headland reaches nearly 250 feet above sea level and from the North Cornwall Coast Path which traverses it there are magnificent views along this imposing coastline.

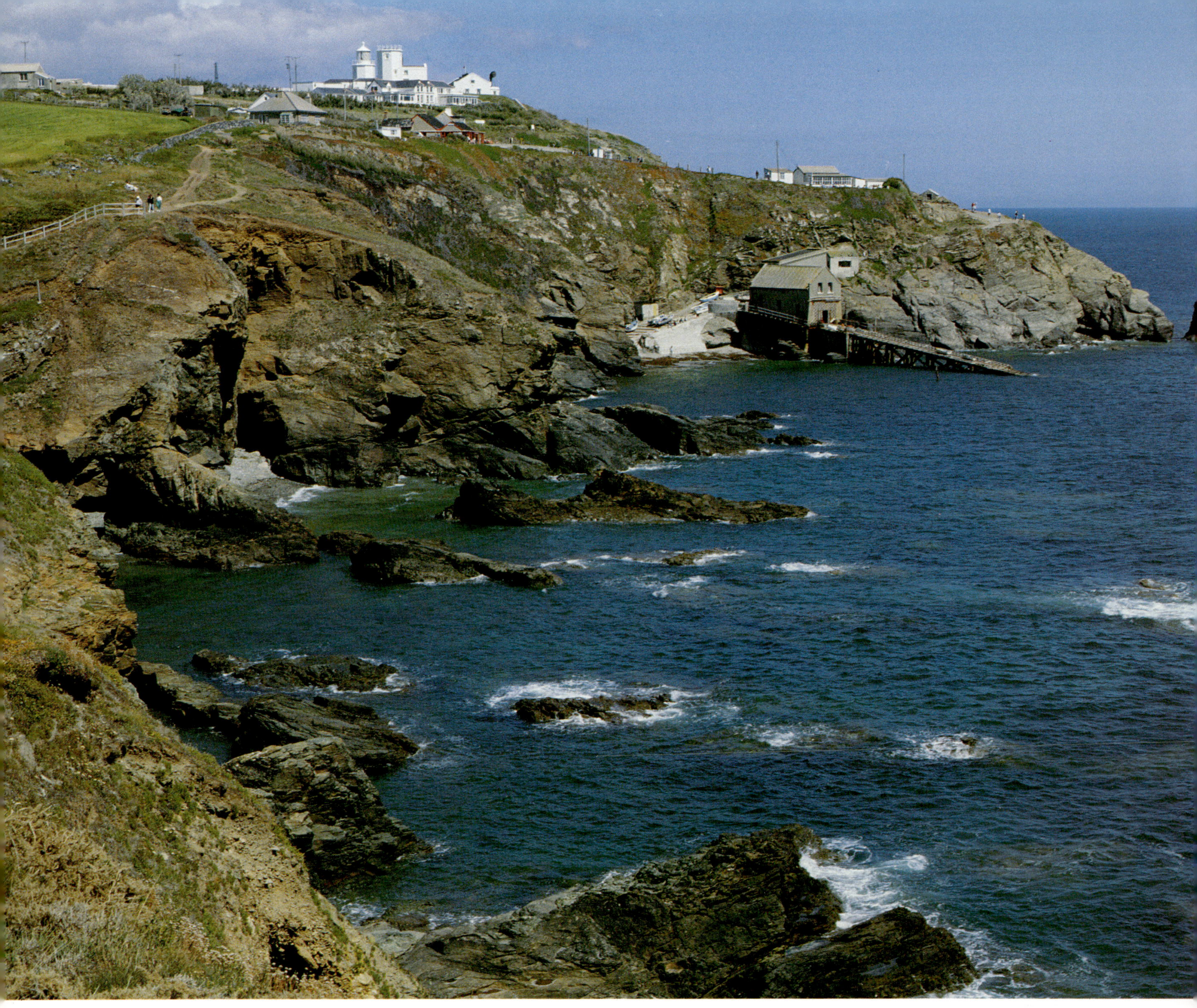

Lizard Point. The most southerly point of mainland Britain, the Lizard is so called from the Cornish words 'lis' and 'ard' meaning 'high place'. It was the site of Cornwall's first lighthouse, erected in 1619 to warn sailors away from the rugged cliffs and rocky coastline which for centuries has been notorious for shipwrecks. The present light has a range of up to 19 nautical miles.

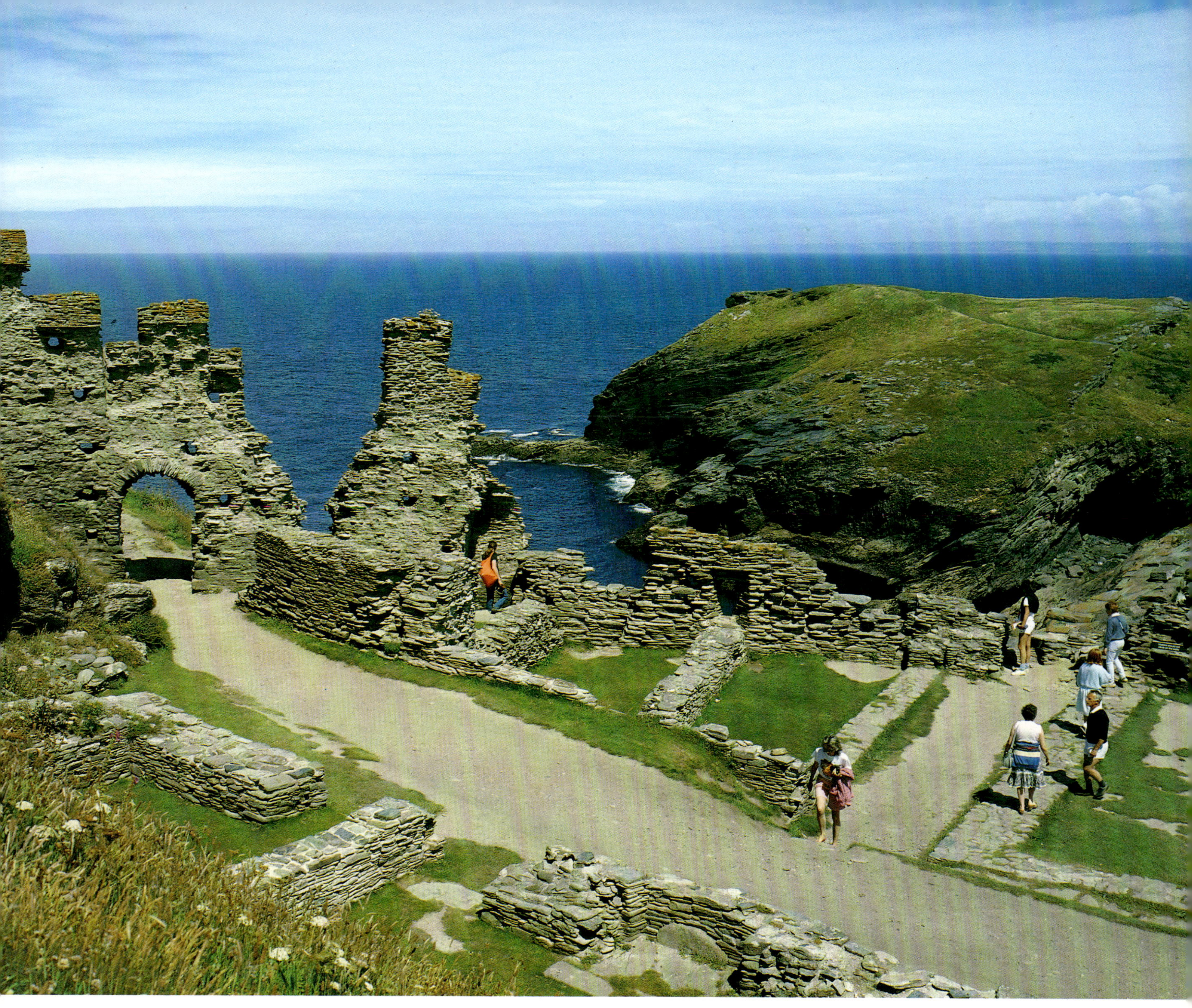

King Arthur's Castle, Tintagel. Situated on a wild and rugged stretch of the Cornish coast where Barras Nose juts out into the Atlantic, Tintagel is famous for its associations with the legends of King Arthur and his Knights of the Round Table. Although the earliest parts of the present castle date only from about 1145, the remains of an ancient Celtic monastery survive nearby.

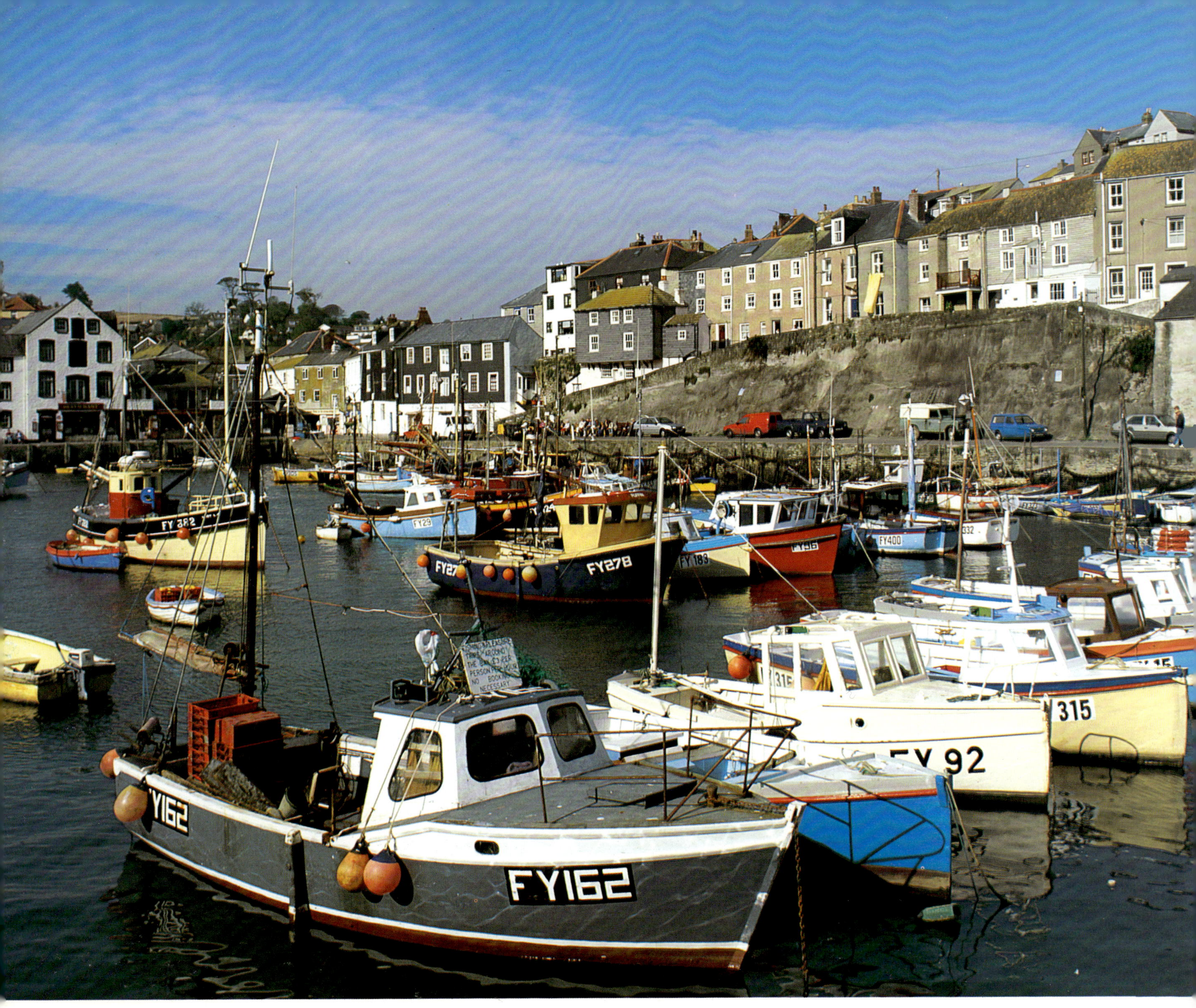

Mevagissey. This picturesque village, which lies in a sheltered position within Mevagissey Bay, was established as a fishing port in the Middle Ages and became an important centre for the pilchard fisheries. Although the trade has declined in modern times the colourful inner harbour, surrounded by narrow streets and twisting alleyways, is still busy with fishing boats and other small craft.

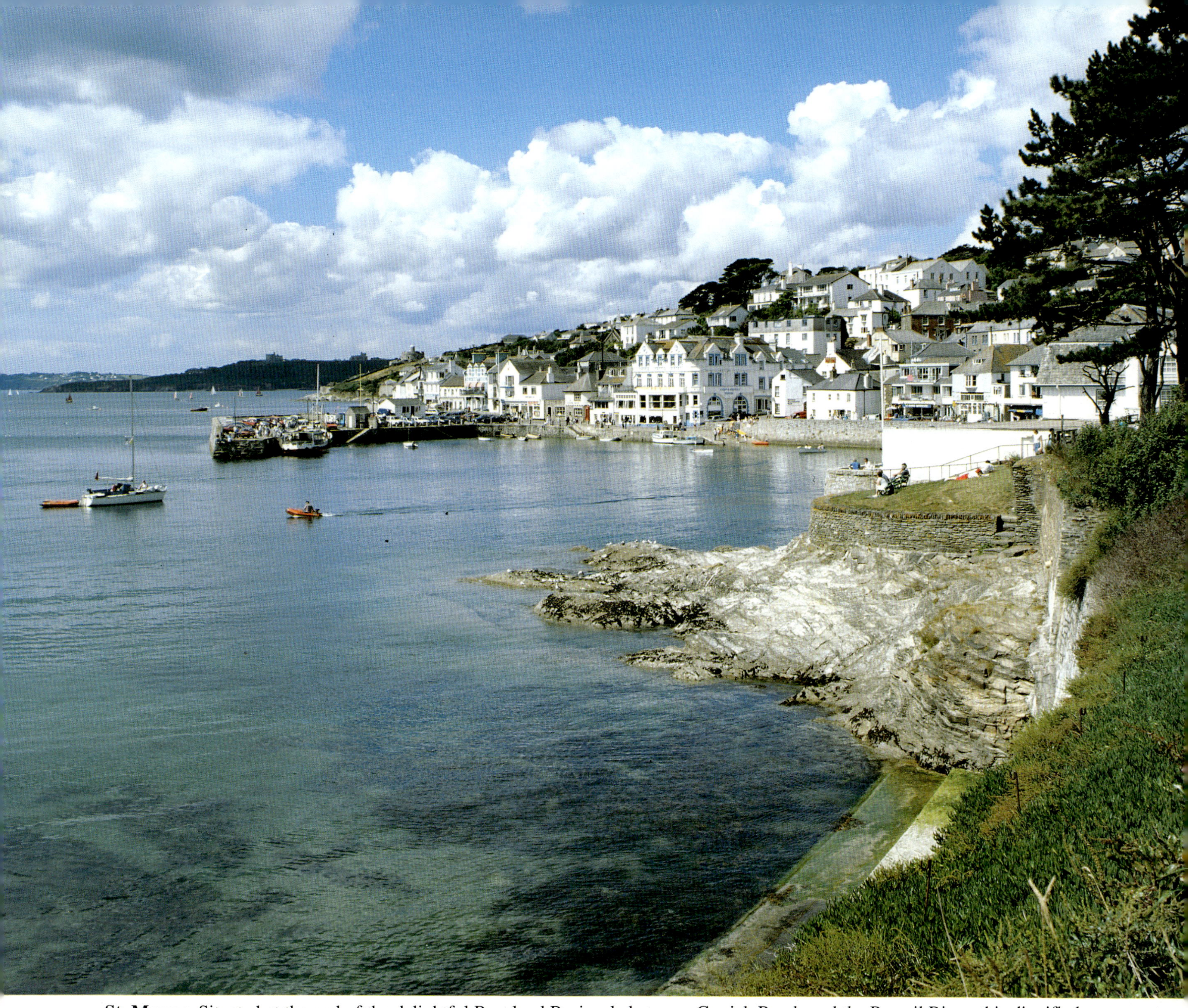

St. Mawes. Situated at the end of the delightful Roseland Peninsula between Carrick Roads and the Percuil River, this dignified little resort is a fine centre for boating activities of all kinds. Built up in terraces and well protected both from the north and the south, St. Mawes shares the mild climate which has justly earned this part of the coast the title of Cornish Riviera.

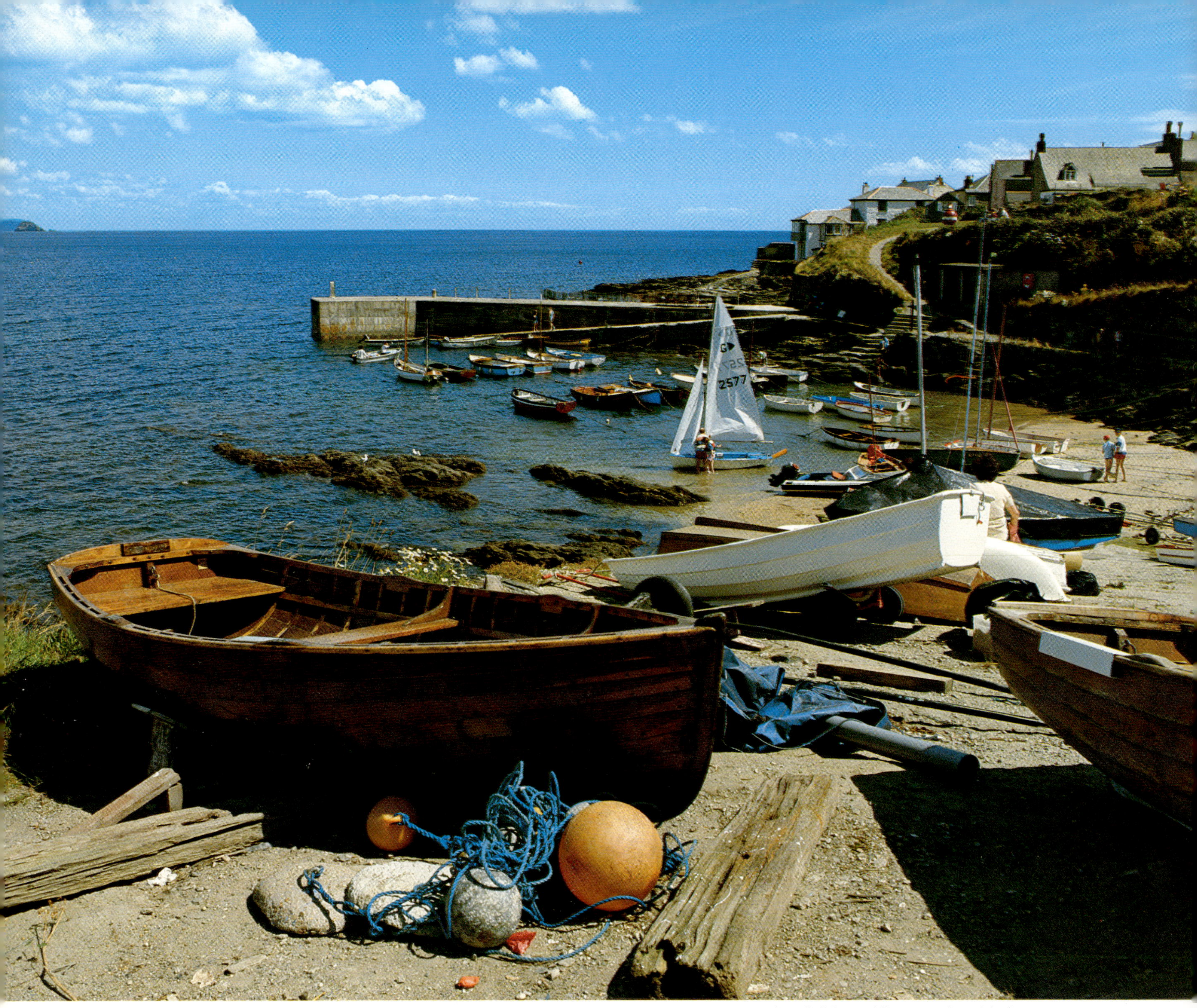

Portscatho. Like many other resorts in South Cornwall, Portscatho was once a quiet fishing village and, with its narrow streets and tiny harbour, it still retains a tranquil atmosphere. Facing east across Gerrans Bay it was once an important centre of the mackerel industry but the boats which crowd into the harbour now are mainly used for pleasure.

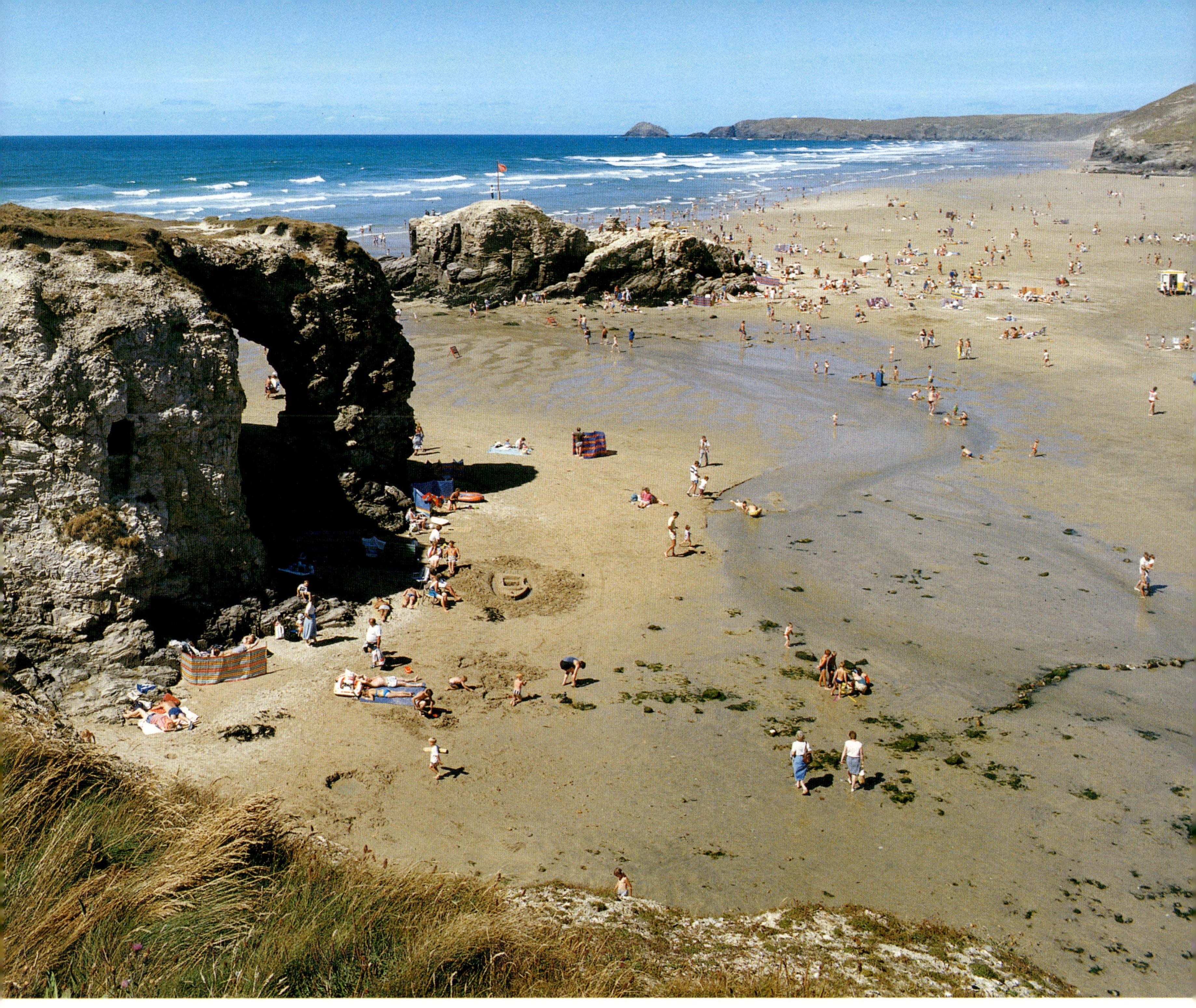

Perranporth. Named after St. Piran who built his first church here, this popular resort is known for its magnificent stretch of firm sand which extends for more than two miles and at the southern end of the beach stand the famous Arch and Chapel rocks. Together with some excellent surfing, the combination of sand, sea, cliffs and caves makes this one of the finest beaches in Cornwall.

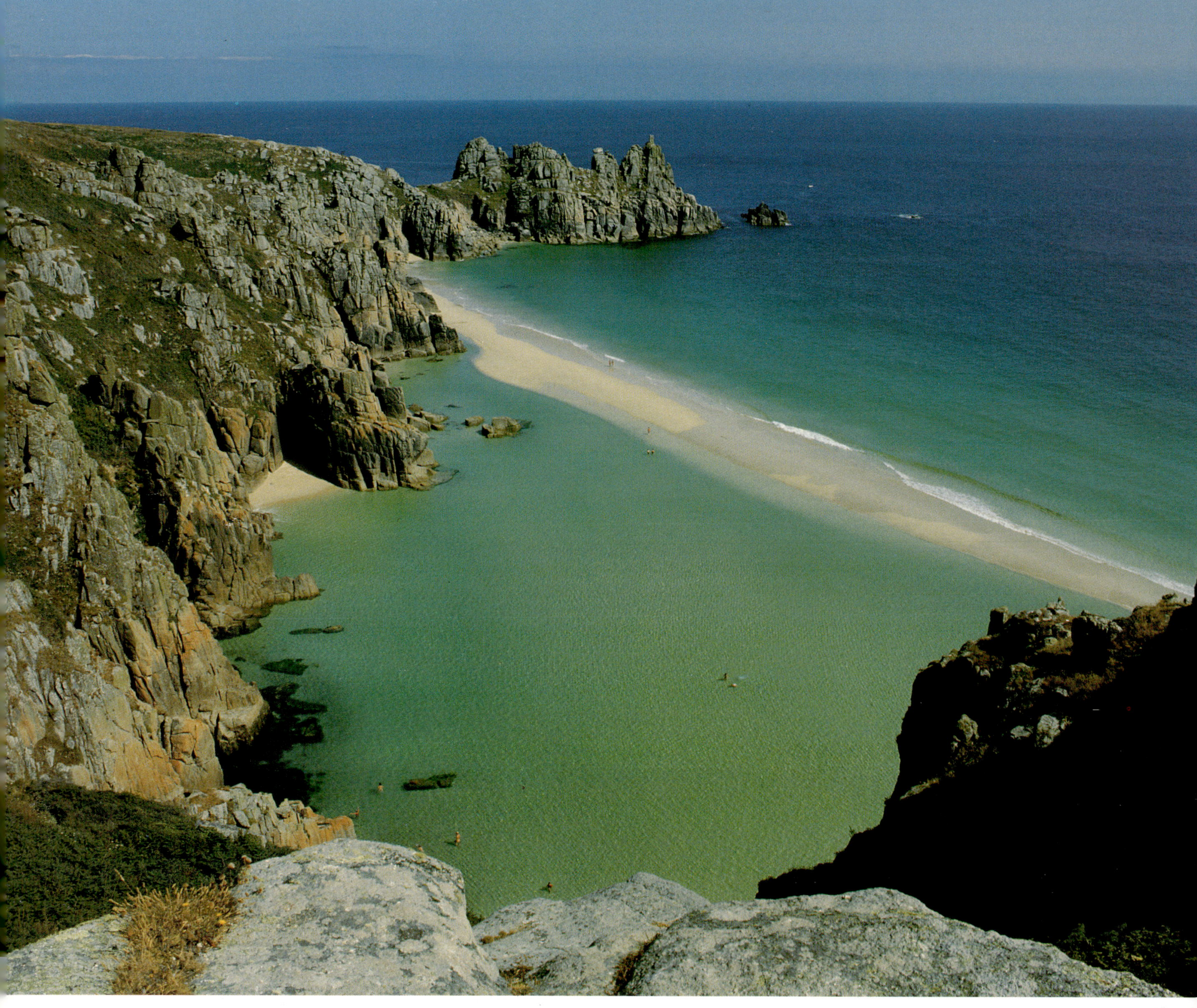

Porthcurno. This beautiful little cove of almost white sand is some three miles from Land's End on Cornwall's southern coast. Beyond it can be seen the rocky, once fortified, headland of Treryn Dinas which, like much of the fine coastal scenery in this area, is protected by the National Trust. Balanced on top is the Logan Rock, a giant boulder which is said to weigh 66 tons.

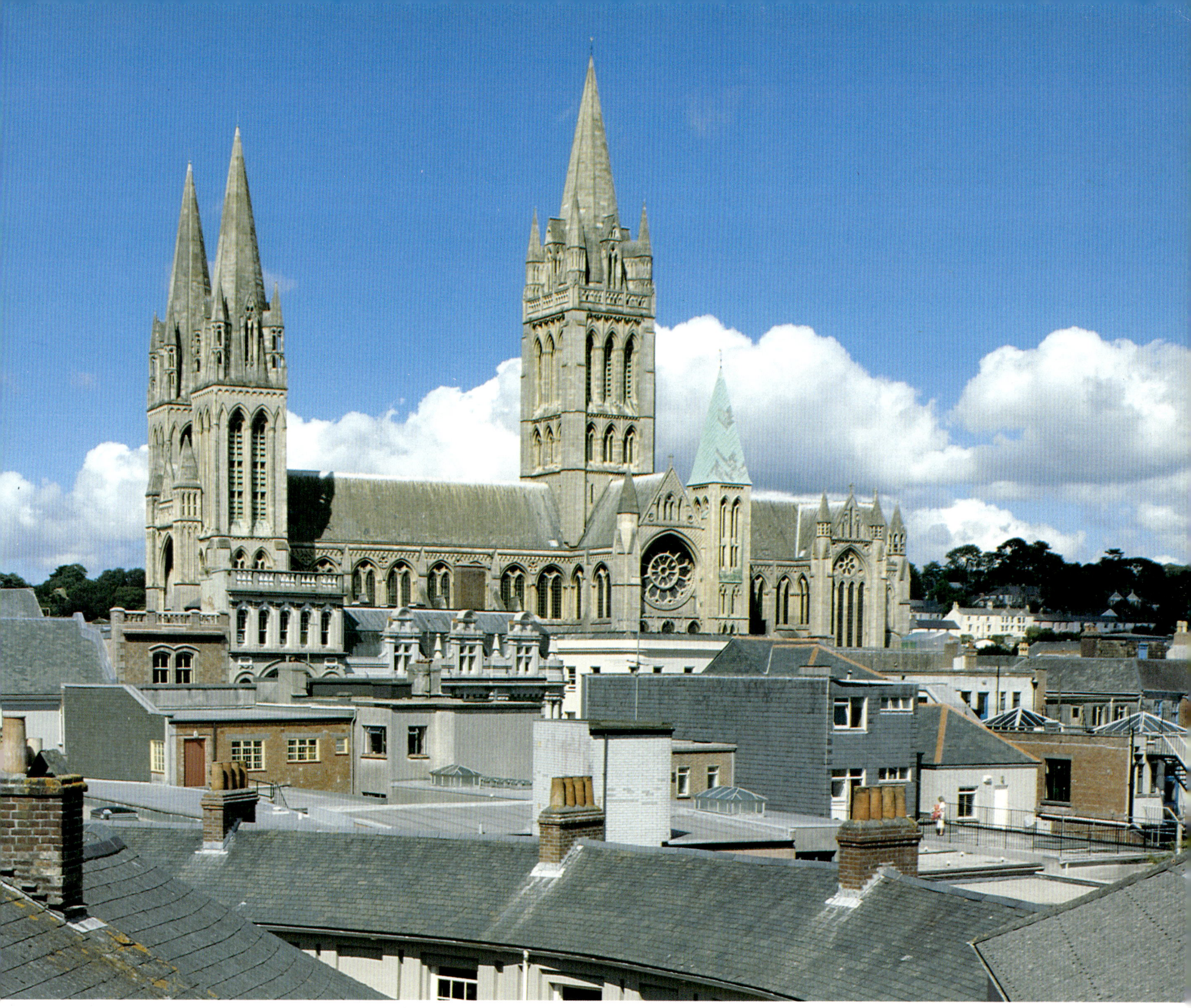

Truro Cathedral. Cornwall's only city, Truro is situated on the Truro River, an arm of the beautiful Fal estuary. The Cathedral, which stands on the site of an older church, was completed in 1910 in the Early English style and blends in well with the Georgian buildings in the surrounding streets. Unusually in an English church, all three towers are crowned by stone spires.

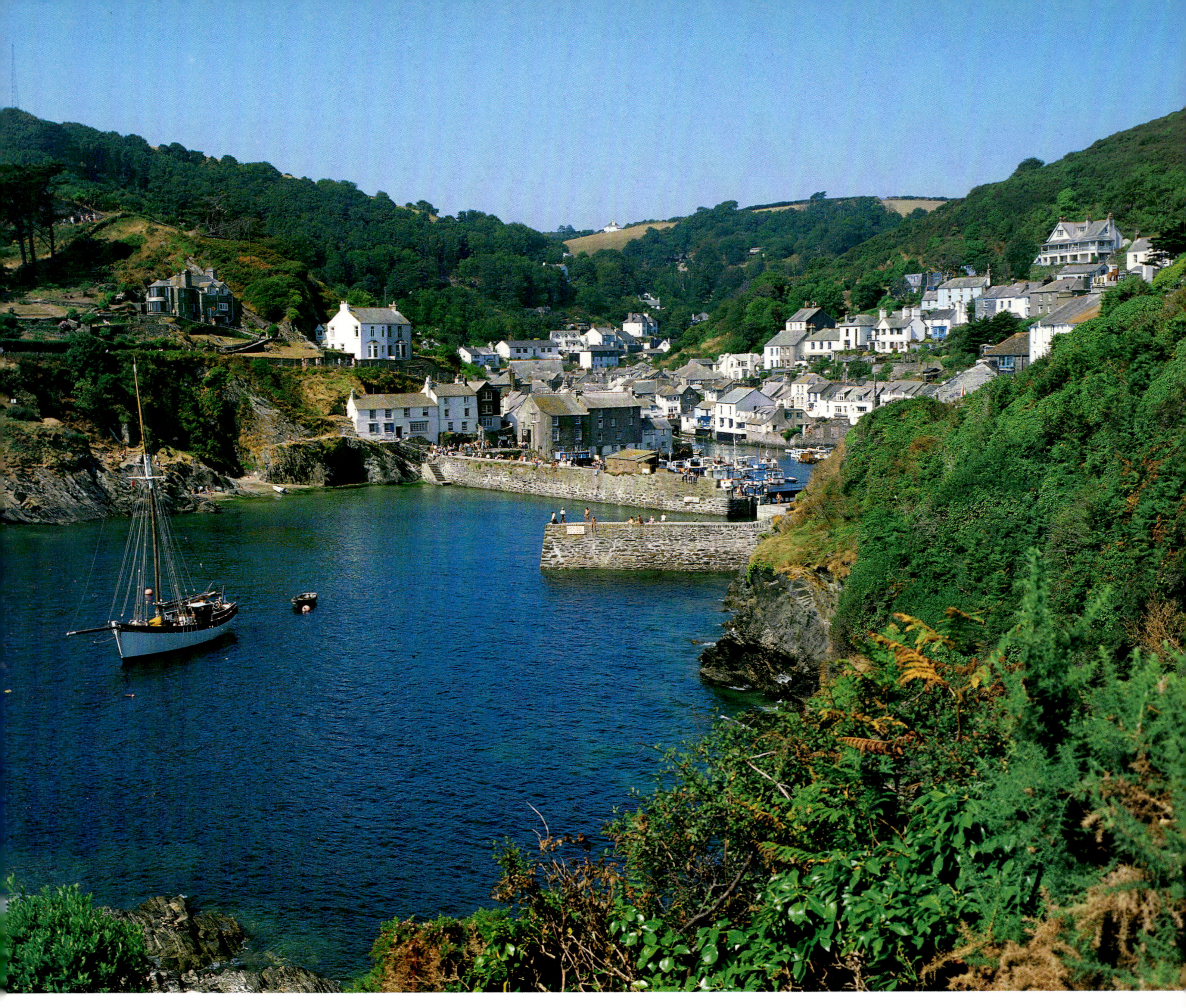

Polperro Harbour. Situated at the foot of a deep wooded combe amid rugged coastal scenery, Polperro is one of England's most attractive and enchanting fishing villages. Ancient white-washed, stone-built cottages, once the homes of smugglers and fishermen, are clustered around the tiny, bustling harbour which provides a safe haven for both fishing boats and pleasure craft.

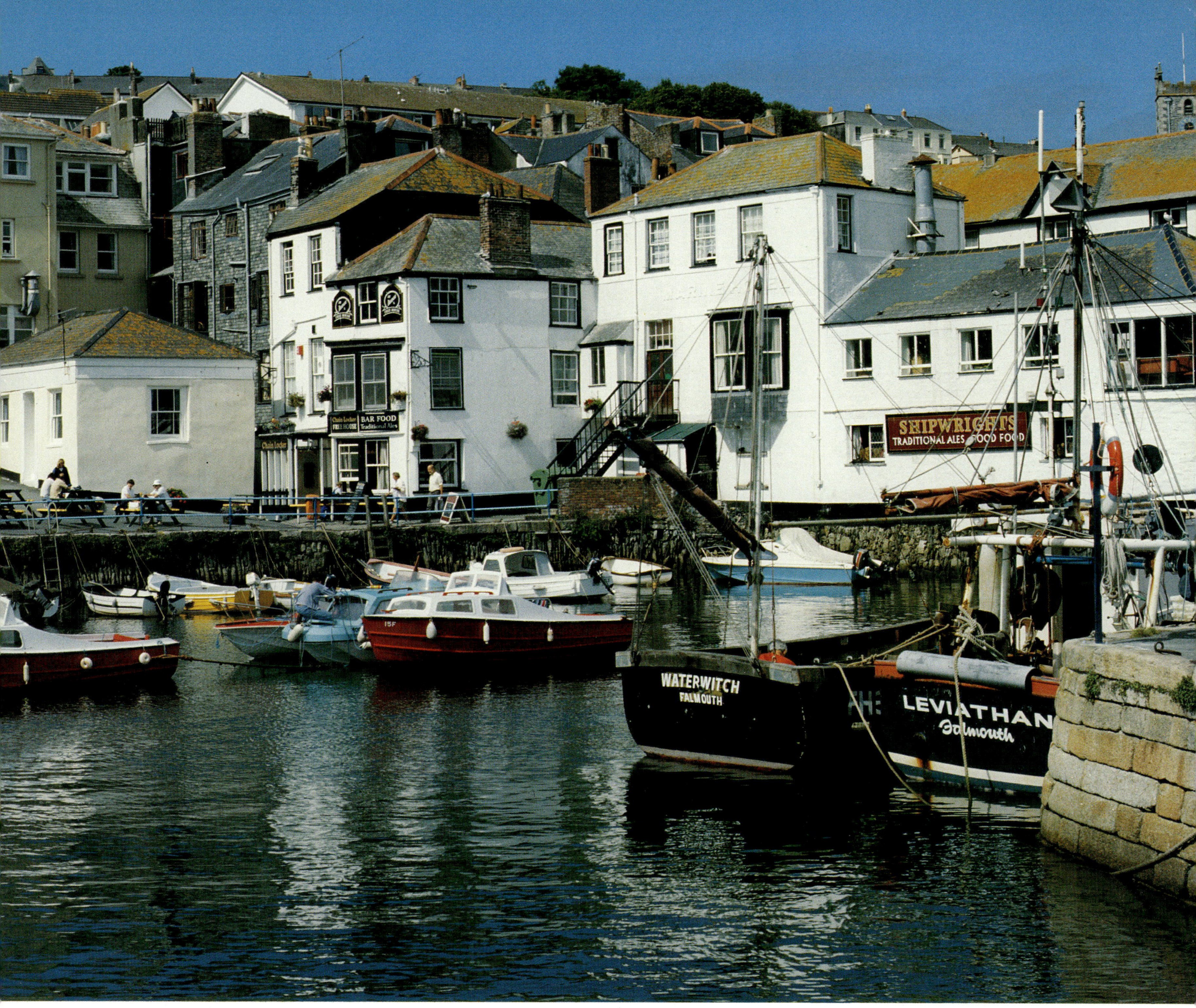

Custom House Quay, Falmouth. Now a popular holiday centre Falmouth has been a flourishing port for over 200 years with one of the finest natural harbours in the world. The old part of the town grew up around Custom House Quay which was built in the 17th century. Here excise officers used to burn contraband tobacco in a special furnace which still stands near the entrance to the quay.

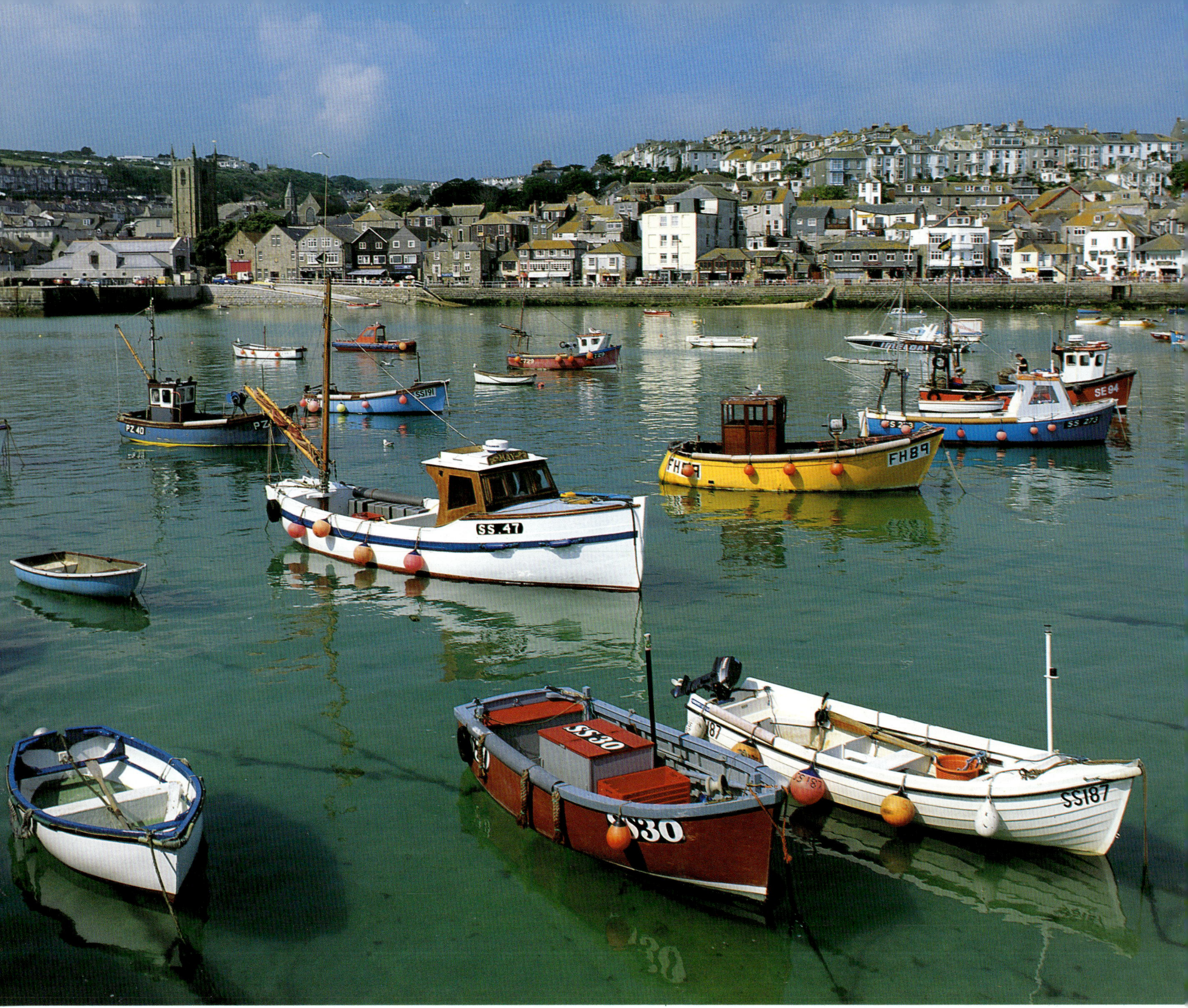

St. Ives Harbour. Once one of Cornwall's major ports, the harbour is still at the centre of life in St. Ives and the oldest part of the town which surrounds it retains much of its old-world charm. This delightful maze of narrow streets and picturesque buildings has attracted artists since the 19th century and many of the ancient fishermen's houses have now been converted into studios.

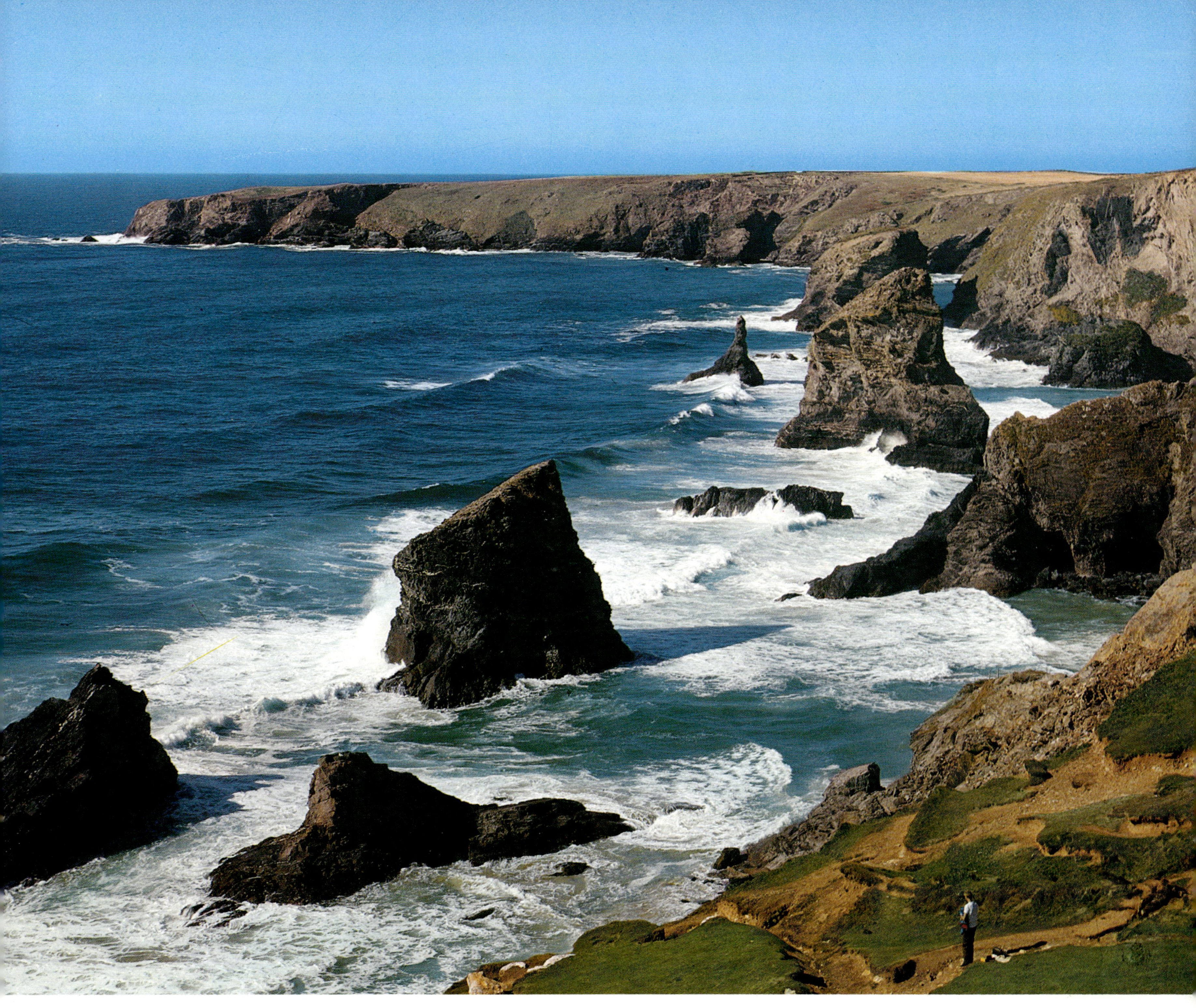

Bedruthan Steps. With its high cliffs and spectacular rock formations Cornwall's Atlantic coast is one of the most memorable stretches in Britain. Legend has it that Bedruthan Steps, the detached off-shore rocks created by the action of the sea, were the stepping-stones of a Cornish giant and a steep flight of steps leads down to them from the grassy cliff-top at Carnewas.

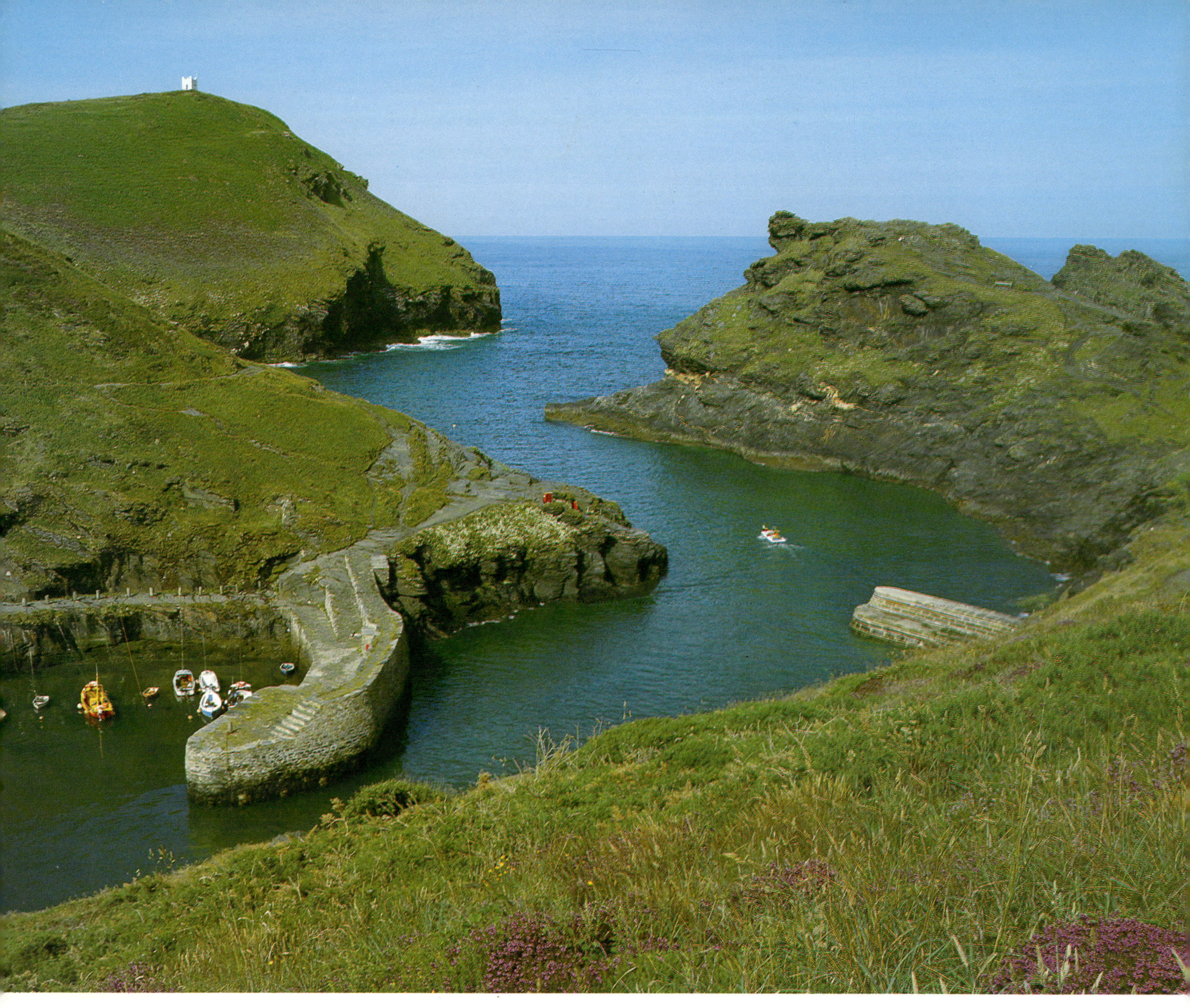

Boscastle. The tiny River Valency winds through a sheltered valley from the high moors towards the little harbour which was once busy with sailing ships loading slate from the local mines. Sturdy cottages cling to the hillside above the deep, rock-enclosed harbour which now provides one of the few refuges from the stormy seas which batter the North Cornwall coast.

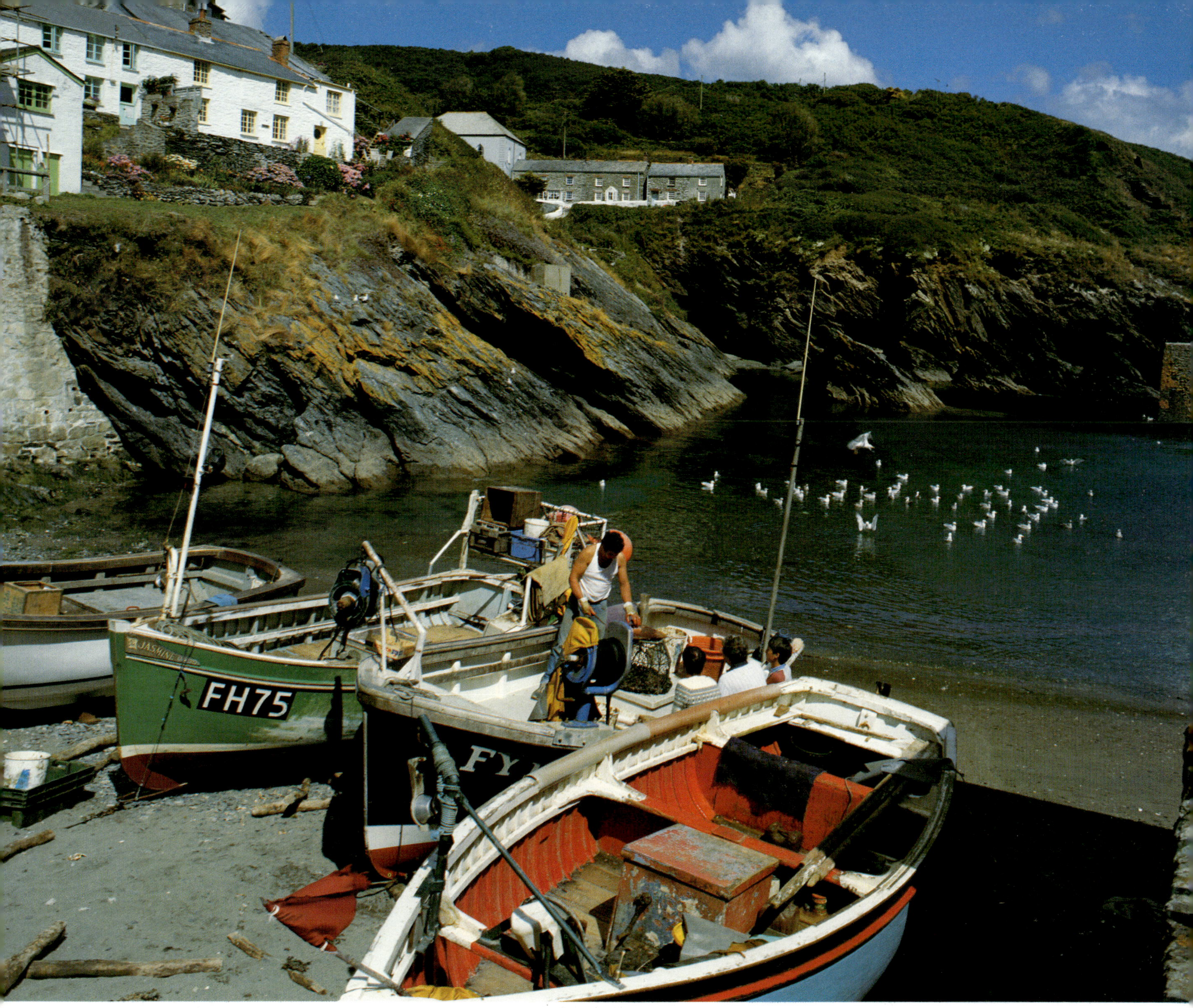

Portloe. One of Cornwall's many diminutive ports and harbours, this delightful little fishing village nestles in a steep valley running down to a narrow rocky cove where the slipway is still used by fishermen. From the village there are clifftop walks along the Cornwall South Coast Path which offer magnificent views across Veryan Bay as it sweeps round from Nare Head to Dodman Point.

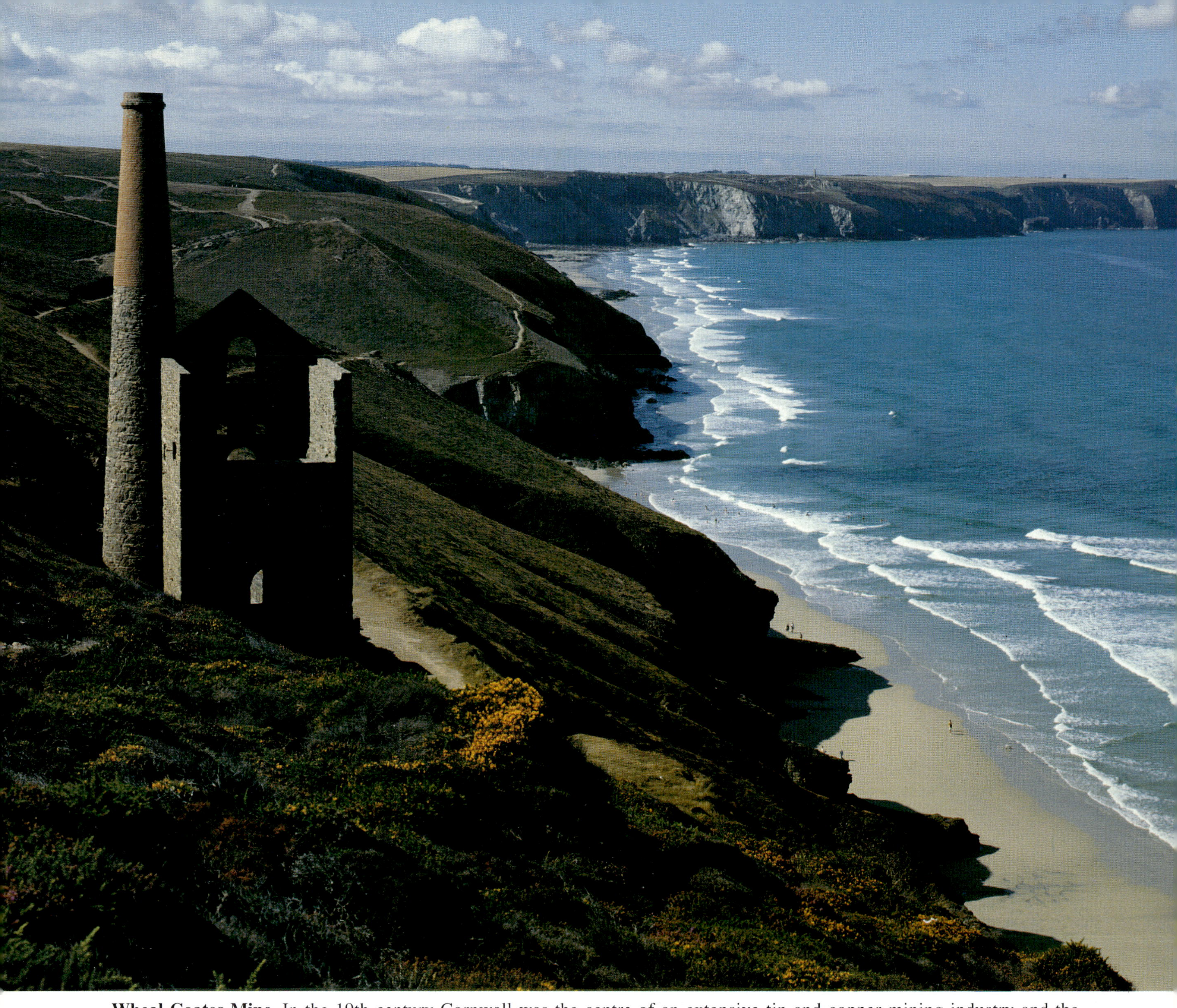

Wheal Coates Mine. In the 19th century Cornwall was the centre of an extensive tin and copper mining industry and the western part of the county is rich in ruined buildings which serve as monuments to this heritage. Among them is the engine house of Wheal Coates Mine which stands amid fine coastal scenery in a dramatic cliff-top position below St. Agnes Beacon.

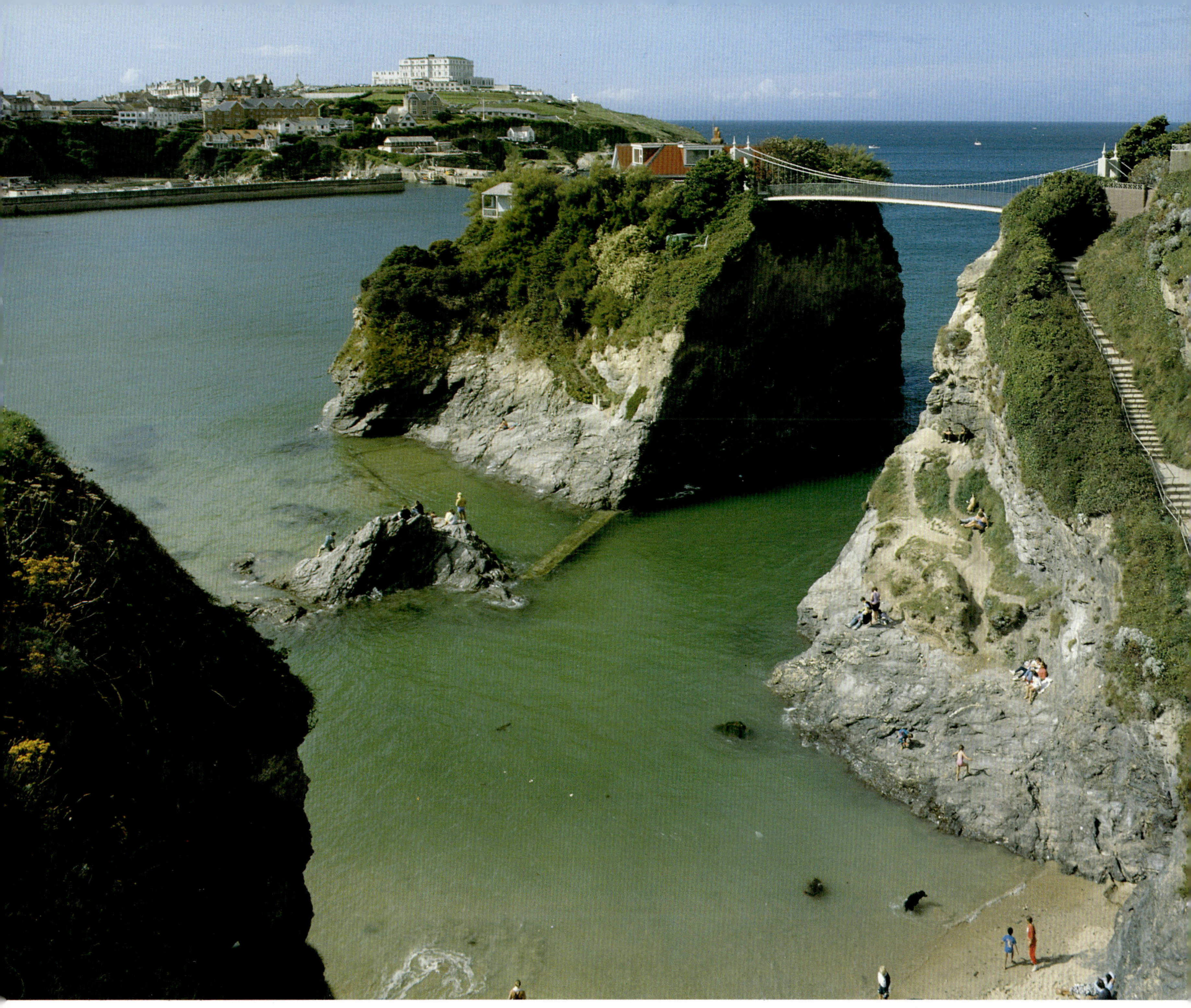

The Island, Newquay. Built on rocky, granite cliffs, Newquay has a number of caves including the Tea Caverns which were used for the storage of smuggled tea. Many of Newquay's sandy beaches are reached by steps or ramps cut into the cliffs and the tiny Island, which lies between Towan Beach and Great Western Sands, is joined to the mainland by a slender suspension bridge.

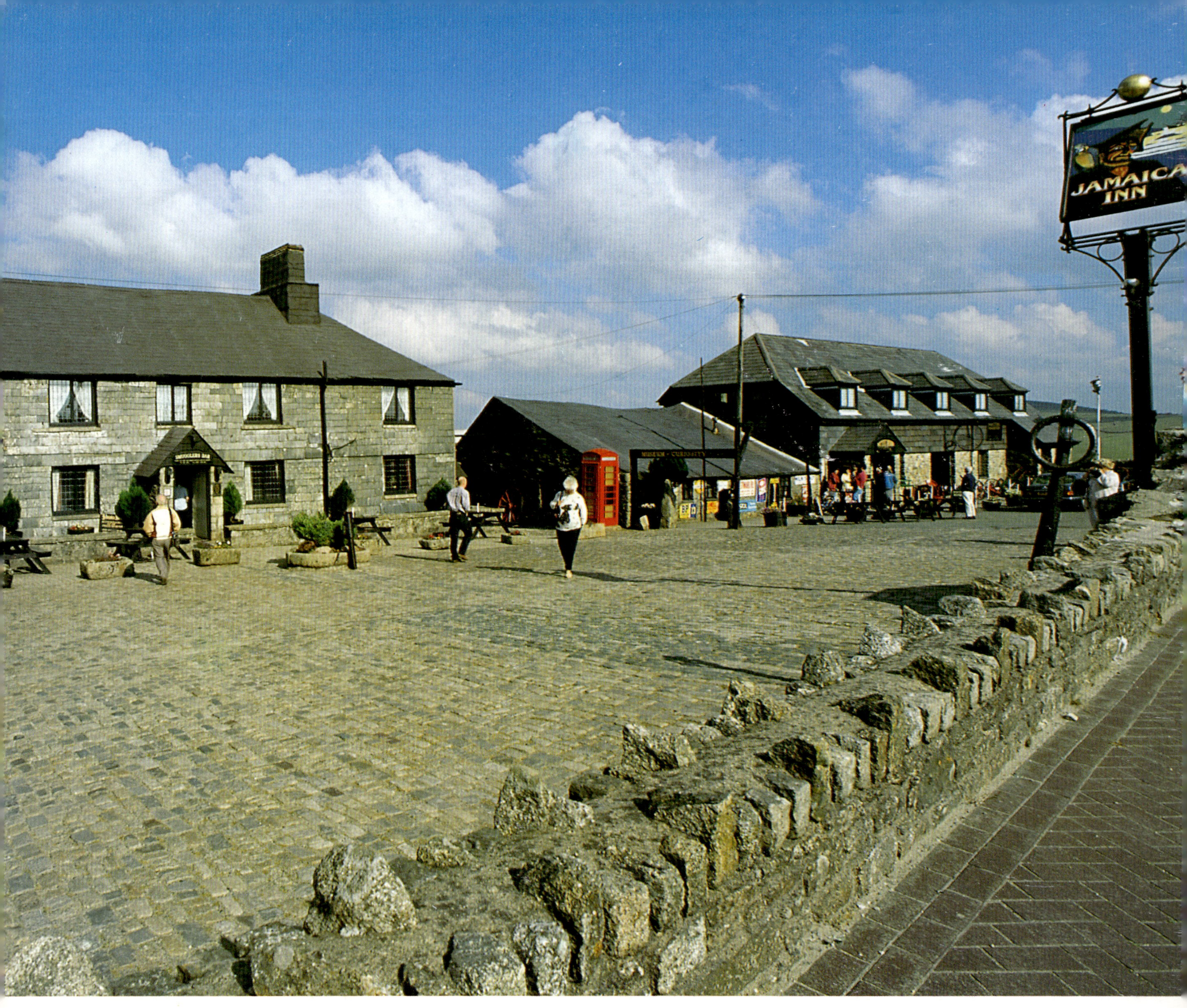

Jamaica Inn. Bodmin Moor consists of more than 100 square miles of wild moorland crossed by streams and studded with granite tors. It is said that smugglers used to store their contraband at Jamaica Inn, made famous by Daphne du Maurier's novel of the same name. It also provided a staging post for the London mail coach on the Bodmin to Launceston road at Bolventor.